The Heather Garden

The
Heather Garden

Harry van de Laar

- **Design**
- **Management**
- **Propagation**
- **Cultivars**

Translated by P. Rowe-Dutton

Adapted and with a Foreword by
DAVID McCLINTOCK

With 47 colour photographs and 21 line drawings

COLLINS 14 St James's Place, London

ISBN 0 00 219737 5

First published in Holland as *Het Heidetuinboek* by Zomer and Keuning
Boeken B.V. in 1974

Filmset by Jolly & Barber Ltd, Rugby, Warwickshire

Printed in Great Britain by Collins Clear-Type Press, London and
Glasgow.

Contents

5

Photographs by   H. M. J. Blum, Steenwijkerwold; H. A. van Daesdonk, Tilburg; H. P. Dijkhuizen, Dronten; J. den Hengst, Aarlanderveen; H. J. van de Laar, Boskoop; Research Station for Arboriculture, Boskoop; G. Seppen, Hilversum; C. J. Swinkels, Borger; M. van Vugt, Oss; M. Zwijnenburg, Boskoop.

Line Drawings by   H. J. van de Laar, Boskoop

List of Plates

Foreword

Mr van de Laar is a very charming man, as a recent letter to me said. But he is much more. He has been on the staff of the Research Station at Boskoop, Holland, in the midst of 1,000 heather nurseries, for twenty years, and is the guiding light on technical matters for Ericultura, the flourishing Dutch Heather Society. Heathers are now probably the main interest of this able plantsman: indeed he must know more about them than anyone else on the Continent. One proof of his knowledge is this book of his, now available in English.

The Dutch original, *Het Heidetuinboek*, appeared in November 1974. Within three years, it had had five editions and no less than 40,000 copies had been sold. In 1976 it was translated into German, as *Heidegärten*, by the eminent dendrologist, Dr Gerd Krüssman. He too is knowledgeable about heathers, and added some of his wisdom to the German version. I am grateful to him for his cooperation and for enabling this English version to benefit from what he added to the German one. Indeed, as a result as well of additions made to the English version, this contains information available in no other book, for example some of the data on the introduction of cultivars and the revised distribution maps.

The literal English translation was made by Miss P. Rowe-Dutton, formerly of the Horticultural Bureau at the East Malling Research Station in Kent. The text, however, required very extensive subsequent adaptation. To give just one or two examples: short though the distance is between our coasts, most of Holland has a Continental climate, much harsher in winter than ours. So the protection essential there is never needed here and the wide range of species we can grow demanded a complete re-writing of p. 38. Their main peat, black peat, does not exist in Britain; while they have to be careful of impure water from their canals which we do not.

But Mr van de Laar's text has been adhered to whenever possible, and the modifications made agreed with him. This is important, for although he gives a full supply of sound, experienced advice, some of his recommendations may surprise British readers. But, based as they are on the immensely successful Dutch horticultural practice, it is well worth seeing if we cannot gain by adopting some of its refreshingly original ideas.

One matter that has been left unaltered is the choice of cultivars. This was partly out of respect for Mr van de Laar's personal choice, partly for the value of the Dutch experience it incorporates, and partly because of the difficulty of deciding where to stop with what might have been added. There is special interest in the cultivars of Dutch origin described here, many of which are very good and as yet little known in this country. At least there can be no doubt about the extreme hardiness of those included, and there are nearly 300 of them. Further ideas can be obtained from books in the Bibliography and from the catalogues of the nursery men listed on p. 152.

This book is greatly to be welcomed, for the ability of its author, its excellent advice and for its insight into Dutch ideas. After all, they do sell us countless thousands of heathers each year.

Platt, Kent, England   DAVID MCCLINTOCK

Preface

May that which is correct remain free from envious detraction;
and the errors of ignorance be set right by the better informed.

DIODORUS SICULUS
'History' Bk 1, Chap 5, Sec 2

Heathers have caught the public interest. In 1963 the Heather
Society was founded: within ten years it had 1000 members. In
1971 the Dutch Heather Society 'Ericultura' was started; it too
now has 1000 members, and 1977 saw the beginning of the
Gesellschaft der Heidefreunde, the German Society. These
Societies exchange information and experience and foster the
study of heathers. They encourage the correct naming of
plants. At the present time nearly 700 different Callunas and
hardy Ericas are on sale in these countries.

I hope that this book may contribute to the knowledge of
heathers, their propagation, the making of heather gardens
and all that is connected with them. A variety of aspects has
been dealt with as fully as possible, the object being to produce
a book which would allow even experienced gardeners to learn
something new. Readers will doubtless find that they are
better acquainted with, or more interested in, some aspects
than others. But I hope that every reader will find something
to his taste; I shall then have achieved my aim.

I should like here particularly to thank Mr B. C. M. van Elk
of the Research Station at Boskoop for his critical reading
of the Dutch text and many valuable additions. On the topics
of soil and manures I was assisted by my colleague Mr Th. G.
L. Aendekerk.

11

Getting to know the various heather cultivars takes time, and many trials have been carried out in the last ten years. This important research has been ably supervised by Mr M. Zwijnenburg. I am very much indebted to him for this. In the municipal heather garden at Driebergen-Rijsenburg, where I have always been warmly welcomed, I have been able to collect a great deal of valuable information.

A special word of thanks is also due to Mr David McClintock, with whom I have kept in close contact for many years on the correct naming of heathers.

I also thank my wife and everyone who has contributed in any way to bringing this book to completion, as well as the publishers for their kind help and for the excellent production of this, the first Dutch book on heathers.

I am aware that errors may have crept in, while some topics may have been omitted that might perhaps have been dealt with. Comments on, and criticisms of, the contents will be gladly received, either direct or through the publishers.

Boskoop, Holland   HARRY VAN DE LAAR

Introduction

Why grow heathers?

Those who do will provide the best recommendations. They know:

1. Heathers can provide a rich and changing variety of colour from foliage, flowers and seed-heads all the year round. Many of the easiest are at their best in the drabbest months.

2. They are versatile evergreens, easy to grow, inexpensive to buy and long-lasting.

3. They can soon provide a weed-free garden, which needs little or no maintenance.

4. They are care-free, and thrive on quite poor soils, including those near the sea, many of them in windy places. Pests and diseases are generally unusual and of no importance. So up-keep costs are none, or at least negligible.

5. There are hundreds of bone-hardy variants in many colours, sizes, shapes and characters to choose from.

6. They are easily propagated, so replacements can be provided at no cost.

7. Attractive forms can regularly be found in the wild, which are similarly easily propagated from cuttings with no detriment to the original plant.

8. Many make excellent cut flowers, and dry well for the winter.

9. Their fascination: they get you!

13

Soil

Many people are under the impression that heathers will grow on any type of soil. They may have noticed that wild heather grows on even very poor ground and may therefore think it unnecessary to improve the soil in their garden. This is not so. Most ericaceous plants must have an acid soil if they are to grow and flower well. In addition to the acidity, the water-holding capacity, drainage, aeration and nutrient status of the soil are all of importance.

The soil on our moors, however poor, generally has the right degree of acidity; this and other factors make it the ideal environment for this sort of vegetation. Garden soils, on the other hand, may have unsuitable acidity, moisture and nutrient conditions. For example some collections, planted in unsuitable conditions, have been lost from drought. A dry period in spring, followed by low rainfall, has caused the death of part, or often the whole, of beds of heathers that had been growing excellently and flowering abundantly. Such disasters are frequently the result of unsuitable soil composition; it contains too little organic matter, so that it cannot hold enough water.

The most suitable soils for heathers are sandy and peaty ones. The acidity of peaty soils is usually right; moreover, they contain plenty of organic matter. Sandy soils, on the other hand, may be too chalky and contain only a small amount of organic material.

In short, to keep heathers in good condition,

1. the *acidity* of the soil must be right;
2. the soil must contain enough *organic matter*; and
3. the fungi and bacteria with which heather roots live in *symbiosis* must be present.

Let me comment on these three terms.

Acidity

The acidity of the soil can be measured with a pH meter or soil indicator and is expressed in terms of pH. A pH of 7 is neutral. Somewhat surprisingly a lower figure indicates a higher degree of acidity. For example, pH 3 which is very low means a very high degree of acidity.

The pH can be assessed most quickly by an informed glance at the local natural vegetation, including weeds. Thus Sheep's Sorrel (*Rumex acetosella*) is a sure indicator of acidity, Traveller's Joy (*Clematis vitalba*) of some chalk. It can also be determined by soil analysis. This can be done fairly simply by anybody with a soil testing outfit, but it might be more reliable to have the soil analysed by the County Horticultural Officer (usually based at the County Agricultural/Horticultural College) or by the local Ministry of Agriculture Officer, when the lime requirement, the soil texture and the available phosphorus, potassium and magnesium can also be determined.

The most suitable degree of acidity or pH for ericaceous plants is:

a. in peaty soils, between 4 and 4.5;
b. in sandy soils, between 4.5 and 5;
c. in sandy clay soils, under 5.

If water movement in the soil is unsatisfactory, this must be improved by drainage. On certain acid soils this may mean breaking up the hard pan, the impermeable horizon which often forms about 40 cm below the surface.

Clay and dune soils generally have a higher pH. There is

usually some lime in them (it comes from shells in dunes), but they may be all right for winter heaths. Even after adding woodland soil or peat however, the pH may remain too high to allow good growth and flowering of many other ericaceous plants. Old dunes are an exception, because their surface soil can become sufficiently leached to be able to grow heathers.

Organic matter

Organic matter (often wrongly called humus) is very important. The amount that is present in the soil determines the moisture-holding capacity and, ultimately, the amount of moisture that is available during a dry period. Moreover, organic matter may hold nutrients. This happens with material that has decomposed to such an extent that it has turned into humus, that is to say, the plant remains are no longer recognizable as such.

Organic matter is essential for heathers and other ericaceous plants. Peat soils are rich in organic matter. Sometimes they contain 40–45%; in raised bogs it can even reach 90%.

Sandy soils on which organic manure (for example, farmyard manure) is used regularly generally have an organic content of 3–7%. Poor sandy soils are not very suitable for a heather garden and clay soils also contain little or no organic matter. Moreover they are often too stiff. But both can be adapted with proper treatment.

In natural conditions humus is formed from, among other things, fallen leaves. This also happens in heather gardens. Heathers are very shallow-rooting, utilizing the uppermost layers of soil. They keep forming new feeding roots in the top layer of humus, which, over the course of years, is produced by the plants themselves.

Symbiosis

Another reason for the importance of organic material is that it encourages fungal and bacterial activity. In all soils, but particularly in soils rich in humus, there are to be found all sorts of soil fungi (mycorrhiza) and bacteria that live in symbiosis with the root hairs of ericaceous plants. Symbiosis means the condition in which an organism lives on, or even inside, another to the advantage of both of them. Not only the Ericaceae, but also many other plants, such as beech (*Fagus*), sea buckthorn (*Hippophae*) and many conifers, live in symbiosis with soil fungi. Seed-beds of beech and pine (*Pinus*), for example, are 'inoculated', before sowing, with soil that contains the fungi necessary to these plants.

If there is little or no organic matter in the soil, there will be little symbiotic activity. The plants will not thrive and may gradually wither away.

Improving the soil

The soil in a garden can vary from place to place. It may well be that certain parts are suitable, or can be made so, for the culture of ericaceous plants, while other parts are not, or can only be made so with difficulty. Nevertheless people may still want, for practical and aesthetic reasons, to grow heathers. If so, the soil can be improved by the addition of the following.

Woodland soil

This is the top layer of soil from coniferous or deciduous woods. The loose material is collected mainly from below pine trees, when it is called pine needle litter or coniferous litter. The organic content of this is high and the pH low (below 3.5). Woodland soil contains a moderate amount of nutrients and is low in salts. It is particularly suitable for improving wet soils and those that are too compact. Moreover, since it lowers the pH, it is useful for heathers and related plants. Normally a quantity of 2 to 3 m^3 per 100 m^2 is applied.

Leaf mould

The composition of leaf mould can vary greatly, depending on the sort of leaves that it consists of and on the soil they come from. The pH is generally higher than that of woodland soil or peat. The nutrient content is also higher. Leaf mould – in many cases consisting of beech and oak leaves – is very suitable for soils that are susceptible to drought because it can hold a great deal of water. The amount to use is 2 to 3 m^3 per 100 m^2.

Peat

Peat, usually moss or sphagnum peat, has a low pH which makes it also excellent for reducing the pH, but it is deficient in nutrients so it is necessary when using it to add extra nitrogen, 0.5 kg of nitrochalk per m^3. It also improves the air-water ratios of wet soils. This has the effect of increasing the moisture holding capacity of the soil which can be very beneficial on soils susceptible to drought. When it is used, the subsoil must be very permeable. Peat is particularly useful in dealing with high pH soils, such as clay soils with a high content of calcium carbonate. In these cases the main danger is chlorosis (see p. 20). Reduce the pH by mixing a substantial quantity of peat (5 to 10 m^3 per 100 m^2) with the top soil (for example with a rotary cultivator). A fresh layer of peat or woodland soil must then be applied regularly. Then in dry periods apply water; iron and manganese are more readily available in a moist soil.

Manures and fertilisers

Soils on which a heather garden is to be planted may need to be improved, not only by the addition, for example, of peat; in Holland we have often found it helps to apply manure too. This applies both to soils not previously planted with heathers and to the already established heather garden.

Before planting

There is, of course, a great difference between a garden planted on arable land that has been regularly well manured and one on soil that has not been manured for many years. In the latter case, one would do well, before planting, to work a certain amount of farmyard manure into the top soil.

When heathers are to be planted in the spring, it is advisable to dig the soil in the previous autumn or during the winter and to manure it at the same time. For this purpose old, rotted cow manure is very suitable, at the rate of 300 to 400 kg per 100 m². A greater quantity of manure can damage the plants. There is little or no point in incorporating the manure deeper than 30 cm. On the other hand, if it is too near the surface, there is a very great danger of scorching the roots.

If farmyard manure is not available or is difficult to get, dried cow, or chicken, manure may be used instead. These products, available in sacks, should be spread at the rate of 30 and 15 kg per 100 m² respectively.

In the absence of a full soil analysis, it is often best to take the precaution of applying a magnesium-containing fertiliser (kieserite) at the rate of 5 kg per 100 m², and working it into the soil. If magnesium is known to be deficient, a quick response can be obtained by spraying with 2% Epsom salts in water at fortnightly intervals throughout the summer. Sandy soils, in particular, often seem to have a low magnesium content. In general it can be assumed that, with the amount of

19

farmyard manure recommended above, enough potash and phosphorus will have been given to last for 1–2 years.

When large quantities of peat have been used in the preparation of the soil, extra trace elements should be applied. This is probably most conveniently done by using a foliar feed that contains such important minor elements as magnesium, copper, boron, cobalt, zinc, manganese and molybdenum.

There are a few sandy soils that are too acid for heathers to do well. In this case it is advisable to apply some chalk.

In an established heather garden

Deciding whether or not to manure an established heather garden requires judgment. If, after two or three years, the plants have not yet formed a close cover, it may be advisable to sprinkle dried cow or chicken manure over the soil, at a rate of 15 kg or $7\frac{1}{2}$ kg per 100 m² respectively. On dry soils it is particularly important to manure the ground in good time, about the middle of March. It is beneficial to work the manure into the surface soil (taking care that heather seedlings and surface roots are not damaged).

On the other hand, the plants may be held back, not by lack of nutrients, but because the top layer of soil dries out too much during rainless periods. In this case an additional dressing of manure can even further impede the uptake of moisture by the plants. It is the water supply that is causing the trouble, and we must start to water (see p. 33). Indeed in general it is best to see first if a good drenching with water is not what is required. The use of artificial fertilisers is not recommended, because it will often make the plants grow too fast and lack sturdiness.

A yellow discoloration of the foliage (chlorosis) can sometimes develop, particularly on soils that are too calcareous, or locally where, for example, lime was dumped during the building of a house; it is the result of insufficient uptake of iron or, sometimes, manganese. To cure this discoloration, water with a proprietary compound containing the iron chelate Fe-EDDHA (Chel-138 Fe), at the rate of 2 or 3 g per 2 or 3 litres of water per m². In order to avoid leaf damage, it is best applied with a watering can (without a rose) between the plants. Immediately afterwards the plants must be washed with a generous amount of water. This water is needed also to wash the chemical down to the roots. If necessary the treatment may be repeated after 6 to 8 weeks. If, however, after one or two treatments the yellowing does not disappear, the symptoms are probably due to manganese rather than iron deficiency. In this case watering with manganese sulphate at ½ g per litre of water per m² is required. If necessary the treatment may be repeated after 6–8 weeks. Iron and manganese deficiencies cause identical symptoms in heathers.

Again, it is best to try watering as an initial remedy. Keeping the soil moist, gives a better uptake of nutrients. Another way of avoiding chlorosis is to plant the more calcareous parts of the garden with only cultivars of *Erica carnea, E.* × *darleyensis* or *E. erigena*. These winter-flowering heathers are the most tolerant of lime.

However, it is better to treat the soil before planting, so that the risk of iron or manganese deficiency is avoided or reduced to a minimum (see under Peat p. 18).

Design

A heather garden is one that has been laid out in a more or less natural fashion and planted mostly with species and cultivars of heather. In a small garden, heathers can, with advantage, occupy the greater part of the space. In Holland we prefer a heather garden not to border on a smoothly-mown lawn. They should be separated by some barrier, such as a yew hedge or a bed of shrubs, and the same is true when a border of annual flowers, herbaceous perennials and/or bulbs is planned. All this depends very much on the situation of the garden as regards light and space. A heather garden can also be separated from the other parts of the garden by a pond or pool. The surface of the water should be about 25 cm below the surface of the adjoining ground. In order to conceal the edge of the pond, it can be planted up with turves or spreading plants, such as *Acaena, Ajuga* and *Erica tetralix.*

Heathers go well with scattered trees or with trees as a background. Here they are set off to full advantage. On unwooded ground, they can be very effective, provided that care is taken to effect a good transition to the surrounding landscape. In very flat areas, this can be achieved by planting tall shrubs, or perhaps by erecting a wooden fence, or by a combination of both, around the site.

A small heather garden between the house and the pavement in a built-up street can be very striking, but it will stand out rather conspicuously from the average small garden in the immediate neighbourhood. Nevertheless, it has a definite character, and not infrequently other people in the district will start to grow heathers. In fact, a heather garden can be made very effectively in front of a block of two or more houses. This type of joint approach to embellishing the neighbourhood is very commendable. Excellent plans can be made for two or more small front gardens so that they appear to make one unit. The possibilities in such a larger area are greater. Of course the residents must be in complete agreement about the lay-out, and must also genuinely want to grow heathers. Heathers can also be satisfactorily combined with a rock garden, provided there is not too bright a mixture of vividly coloured rock plants.

Heathers can be used in many types of garden and a great many plants other than heathers can be planted in a heather garden. When planning a heather garden do not forget height (the 'third dimension').

As has already been mentioned, trees or bushes are ideal surroundings for creating as natural a composition as possible. In Holland some very fine heather gardens have been laid out under old, severely thinned stands of pine trees *(Pinus)*. In a garden like this it is important that, before any heathers are put in, a living entity is created by including, for instance, Douglas fir, larch, yew, birch, Amelanchier and possibly other broad-leaved species.

Plants show to better advantage if the ground is rather sloping and if the differences in height are somewhat accentuated by rocks or by digging in tree trunks or railway sleepers. Variation in height can also be achieved by a heap of soil surrounded by boulders. This may lead to the development of moister and drier patches, which is useful for an extensive collection; take this into account when considering the species to be planted. Do not plant moisture-loving *Erica tetralix* on the higher and drier patches.

Railway sleepers can also be used for the construction of a path (see Plan 3 on p. 27). Turves may also be dug in vertically along the edges of the path. These edges can be concealed naturally by covering them with low or creeping plants.

In smaller gardens the paths can best be surfaced with pine needles or wood chippings. Turves (lying flat), sections of tree trunks, flagstones and round or hexagonal tiles can also be used with very good effect. In large gardens the possibilities for the use of these paving materials are even greater.

Heathers that are grown under trees and receive too little sunlight will never have the vivid leaf colour of those in full sun. In too much shade the plants also flower less freely. For this reason the construction of a heather garden on a site with a northern aspect, and certainly on one in a very shady position, cannot be recommended.

In order to give some indication of how a heather garden can be designed, several plans have been included in this section of the text. I hope they may stimulate some pleasing ideas.

HOUSE

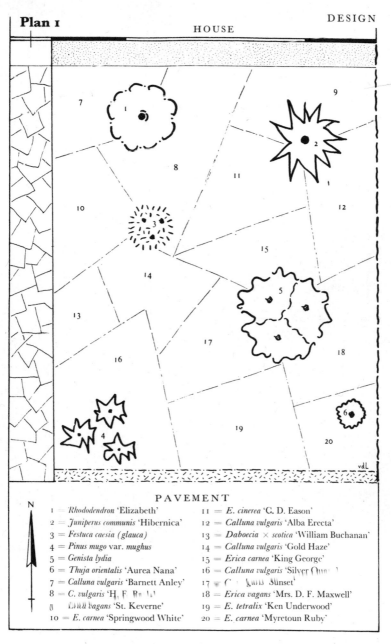

PAVEMENT

N

1 = *Rhododendron* 'Elizabeth'
2 = *Juniperus communis* 'Hibernica'
3 = *Festuca caesia (glauca)*
4 = *Pinus mugo* var. *mughus*
5 = *Genista lydia*
6 = *Thuja orientalis* 'Aurea Nana'
7 = *Calluna vulgaris* 'Barnett Anley'
8 = *C. vulgaris* 'H. E. Beale'
9 = *E. vagans* 'St. Keverne'
10 = *E. carnea* 'Springwood White'

11 = *E. cinerea* 'C. D. Eason'
12 = *Calluna vulgaris* 'Alba Erecta'
13 = *Daboecia* × *scotica* 'William Buchanan'
14 = *Calluna vulgaris* 'Gold Haze'
15 = *Erica carnea* 'King George'
16 = *Calluna vulgaris* 'Silver Queen'
17 = *C. vulgaris* 'Sunset'
18 = *Erica vagans* 'Mrs. D. F. Maxwell'
19 = *E. tetralix* 'Ken Underwood'
20 = *E. carnea* 'Myretoun Ruby'

25

Plan 2

HOUSE

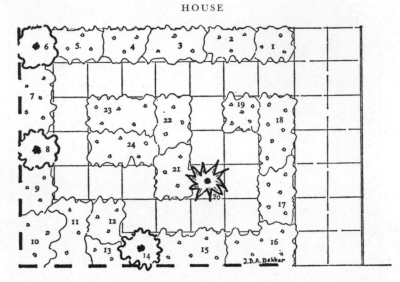

PAVEMENT

Plan of a front garden of 5 m × 3.5 m with washed pebble aggregate paving slabs (50 × 50 cm)

1 = 3 *Erica carnea* 'Snow Queen'
2 = 3 *E. carnea* 'Myretoun Ruby'
3 = 3 *E. carnea* 'Aurea'
4 = 3 *E. tetralix* 'Ken Underwood'
5 = 3 *E. tetralix* 'Alba'
6 = 1 *Rhododendron hippophaeoides*
7 = 5 *Calluna vulgaris* 'Darkness'
8 = 1 *Rhododendron impeditum*
9 = 3 *Calluna vulgaris* 'Tib'
10 = 3 *C. vulgaris* 'Long White'
11 = 3 *C. vulgaris* 'Peter Sparkes'
12 = 3 *C. vulgaris* 'Joy Vanstone'
13 = 2 *C. vulgaris* 'Alportii'

14 = 1 *Rhododendron russatum*
15 = 5 *Erica cinerea* 'C. G. Best'
16 = 5 *E. cinerea* 'Pallas'
17 = 5 *E. cinerea* 'Atrosanguinea Smith's Variety'
18 = 7 *Calluna vulgaris* 'Multicolor'
19 = 5 *C. vulgaris* 'Humpty Dumpty'
20 = 1 *Juniperus virginiana* 'Skyrocket'
21 = 3 *Erica cinerea* 'Cevennes'
22 = 3 *E. cinerea* 'Domino'
23 = 5 *E. cinerea* 'Pink Ice'
24 = 5 *E. cinerea* 'Foxhollow Mahogany'

Plan 3

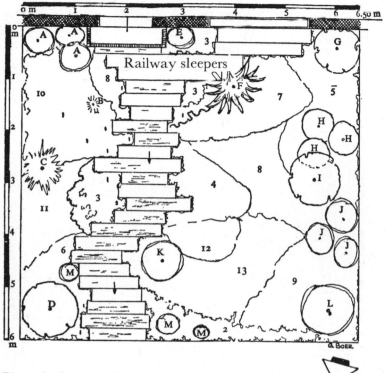

Railway sleepers

Plan of a front garden

A = 3 *Cotoneaster conspicuus*
B = 1 *Pennisetum alopecuroides*
C = 3 *Pinus mugo* var. *mughus*
D = 1 *Betula nana*
E = 1 *Fuchsia magellanica* 'Gracilis'
F = 1 *Juniperus sabina* 'Tamariscifolia'
G = 1 *Pieris japonica*
H = 3 *Rhododendron* 'Scarlet Wonder'
I = 1 *Corylus avellana* 'Contorta'
J = 3 *Salix hastata* 'Wehrhahnii'
K = 1 *Fothergilla major*
L = 1 *Enkianthus campanulatus*
M = 3 *Genista lydia*

1 = 11 *Festuca caesia (glauca)*
2 = 15 *Gaultheria procumbens*
3 = 13 *Vaccinium vitis-idaea*
4 = 9 *Calluna vulgaris* 'H. E. Beale'
5 = 10 *C. vulgaris* 'J. H. Hamilton'
6 = 8 *C. vulgaris* 'Robert Chapman'
7 = 13 *Erica carnea* 'King George'
8 = 17 *E. cinerea* 'C. D. Eason'
9 = 11 *Calluna vulgaris* 'Alba Erecta'
10 = 20 *Erica tetralix* 'Ken Underwood'
11 = 10 *E. carnea* 'Snow Queen'
12 = 5 *Calluna vulgaris* 'Gold Haze'
13 = 18 *C. vulgaris* 'Mrs. Ronald Gray'

27

Plan 4

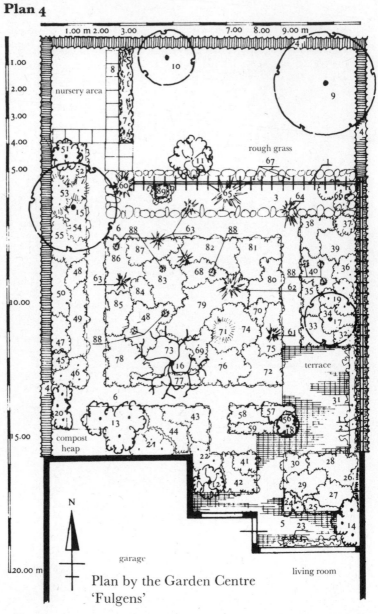

Plan by the Garden Centre
'Fulgens'

1 = pergola (to be covered, for example, with *Clematis* species)
2 = hedge of *Taxus* × *media* 'Hicksii'
3 = rock garden (raised by about 70 cm)
4 = hedge of *Cupressocyparis leylandii*
5 = brick paving
6 = paths of wood chippings
7 = hedge of *Lonicera nitida* 'Elegant'
8 = concrete slabs (50 × 50 cm)
9 = 1 *Sorbus aucuparia* (standard)
10 = 1 *Malus* 'Liset' (standard)
11 = 1 *Decaisnea fargesii*
12 = 1 *Corylus avellana* 'Contorta'
13 = 3 *Fothergilla major*
14 = 3 *Pieris floribunda*
15 = 1 *Betula pendula* (standard)
16 = 1 *Nothofagus antarctica*
17 = 1 *Larix kaempferi* 'Pendula' (standard)
18 = 1 *Ginkgo biloba*
19 = 3 *Salix hastata* 'Wehrhahnii'
20 = 3 *Mahonia aquifolium*
21 = 3 *Fuchsia magellanica* 'Gracilis'
22 = 3 *Skimmia japonica* 'Rubella'
23 = 7 *Polygonum affine* 'Superbum'
24 = 3 *Sarcococca hookeri*
25 = 7 *Hypericum olympicum*
26 = 1 *Jasminum nudiflorum*
27 = 6 *Erica carnea* 'King George'
28 = 8 *Calluna vulgaris* 'Peter Sparkes'
29 = 8 *Daboecia cantabrica* f *alba*
30 = 5 *Dianthus deltoides* 'Splendens'
31 = 10 *Acaena buchananii*
     4 *Calluna vulgaris* 'Alportii'
32 = 3 *C. vulgaris* 'Gold Haze'
33 = 6 *Erica cinerea* 'Cevennes'
34 = 5 *Anemone* × *hybrida* 'Queen Charlotte'
35 = 5 *Erica vagans* 'Mrs. D. F. Maxwell'
36 = 3 *E.* × *darleyensis* 'Darley Dale'
37 = 1 *E. terminalis*
38 = 8 *E. tetralix* 'Ken Underwood'
39 = 5 *E. cinerea* 'C. G. Best'
40 = 5 *Daboecia cantabrica* 'Praegerae'
41 = 5 *Erica carnea* 'Snow Queen'
42 = 7 *Arctostaphylos uva-ursi*
43 = 7 *Erica cinerea* 'C. D. Eason'
44 = 5 *Anaphalis triplinervis*
45 = 1 *Zenobia pulverulenta*
46 = 3 *Rhododendron* 'Elizabeth'
47 = 3 *Calluna vulgaris* 'Gold Haze'
48 = 10 *C. vulgaris* 'Robert Chapman'

49 = 8 *C. vulgaris* 'Mullion'
50 = 5 *C. vulgaris* 'Tib'
51 = 1 *Enkianthus campanulatus*
52 = 3 *Azalea* (Japanese) 'Amoena'
53 = 3 *Pennisetum alopecuroides*
54 = 6 *Empetrum nigrum*
55 = 8 *Erica tetralix* 'Con Underwood'
56 = 3 *Genista lydia*
57 = 3 *Erica cinerea* 'Rosea'
58 = 5 *E. cinerea* 'P. S. Patrick'
59 = 7 *E. tetralix* 'Helma'
60 = 1 *Chamaecyparis obtusa* 'Nana Gracilis'
61 = 1 *Juniperus virginiana* 'Skyrocket'
62 = 1 *Pinus heldreichii* 'Satellite'
63 = 4 *P. mugo* var. *pumilio*
64 = 1 *Juniperus horizontalis* 'Wiltonii'
65 = 1 *J. sabina* 'Tamariscifolia'
66 = 3 *Ilex crenata* 'Golden Gem'
67 = intermixed along the whole border
     9 *Glechoma hederacea* 'Variegata'
     9 *Duchesnea indica*
68 = 6 *Erica cinerea* 'Golden Drop'
69 = 4 *Calluna vulgaris* 'Gold Haze'
70 = 4 *C. vulgaris* 'Golden Carpet'
71 = 3 *Sesleria caerulea*
72 = 9 *Calluna vulgaris* 'Barnett Anley'
73 = 10 *C. vulgaris* 'County Wicklow'
74 = 7 *C. vulgaris* 'C. W. Nix'
75 = 9 *Erica cinerea* 'Atrosanguinea Smith's Variety'
76 = 10 *E. cinerea* 'Pallas'
77 = 12 *Calluna vulgaris* 'Mrs. Ronald Gray'
78 = 11 *C. vulgaris* 'Ralph Purnell'
79 = 16 *C. vulgaris* 'Tenuis'
80 = 7 *C. vulgaris* 'J. H. Hamilton'
81 = 7 *Erica carnea* 'Ruby Glow'
82 = 11 *E. tetralix* 'Hookstone Pink'
83 = 12 *E.* × *darleyensis* 'Silberschmelze'
84 = 5 *E. cinerea* 'Katinka'
85 = 7 *Calluna vulgaris* 'H. E. Beale'
86 = 12 *Erica* × *watsonii* 'H. Maxwell'
87 = 7 *E. vagans* 'Mrs D. F. Maxwell'
88 = 8 *Festuca caesia* (*glauca*)

29

Planting

It is particularly important that the plants should be set out in an intelligent and natural way. Heathers, and many other plants, are frequently planted side by side in a row. This is justifiable in a nursery, but not in a garden. The plants must be set out in such a way that no row (line) is distinguishable in any direction. In nature the plants do not stand in ranks like soldiers; and a heather garden established under unnatural conditions should still look natural.

Planting time

The best time to plant heathers is from mid-September to the end of October and from mid-March to mid-April, except for rooted cuttings. These are better not planted until the end of April or beginning of May. Heathers that are not planted until November-December may not get well rooted, and on peaty soil they can suffer from heaving during a hard frost.

Spacing

The right spacing for heathers depends largely on the species and cultivar (e.g. on whether it grows with a spreading or erect habit), on the type of soil, on the age of the planting material and on the size of the heather garden to be planted. On a poor, sandy soil heathers will undoubtedly grow less quickly, and so are better planted slightly closer together, than on a soil richer in nutrients. Two-year-old plants can, in theory, also be planted closer together than three-year-old material.

In general *Calluna vulgaris* cultivars like 'Mullion', 'Multi-color' and 'Tenuis' should be planted at a distance of 20–30 cm. For those like 'Alba Plena', 'J. H. Hamilton' and 'Tib' a distance of 30–45 cm is enough, while the vigorous 'Alportii', 'H. E. Beale' and 'Long White' can be set 45–60 cm apart.

Forms of *Erica carnea* are mostly planted at 30–45 cm, but the very widely spreading cultivars like 'Springwood White' require 45–60 cm. The cultivars of *E.* × *darleyensis* also cover the ground very rapidly when they are planted 45–60 cm apart.

Nearly all cultivars of *E. ciliaris* can be planted at a spacing of 30–45 cm, as can most forms of *E. cinerea*. The weak-growing 'Alba Minor' and 'Coccinea Smith's Variety', among others, are exceptions, and for these a spacing of 20–30 cm is sufficient. Forms of *E. tetralix* do not grow very rapidly and are happy with 30–45 cm.

The cultivars of *E. vagans* are very variable in habit. Those like 'Lyonesse' and 'Mrs. D. F. Maxwell' can be planted at a distance of 30–45 cm; the weak-growing 'Nana' needs only 20–30 cm, but the vigorous 'Grandiflora', on the other hand, needs 45–60 cm.

Tree heaths, such as *E. arborea* 'Alpina', are often planted singly. When they are grown in a group these heaths should be planted about 1 m apart. Until such a group has joined up, the space between the plants can be very effectively filled with low-growing, summer-flowering heathers, or else, for example, with *Arctostaphylos uva-ursi*, *Empetrum nigrum* and/or *Vaccinium macrocarpon*. Certain herbaceous perennials are also eminently suitable for this purpose.

It should be noted that in small gardens it is advisable to use the closer of the spacings given above. The closer the spacing, the sooner is the soil completely covered, and that is exactly what is wanted. Heathers, like other plants in this family, are very intolerant of sun on the soil around the plant, since their hair roots generally grow just below the surface. In larger areas with more resources in men and money, the wider spacing is to be recommended. The plants will then grow into finer specimens and live longer. But the ground in between will need mulching with peat, or some similar weed-suppressing substance, for longer.

Planting depth

Heather and related plants must be planted at a good depth, certainly deep enough for the root ball to be well below the soil surface. The bottom of the stems must be just under the soil, because the top few centimetres of soil will sink after planting (see Fig. 1). Even if the shoots are slightly below the soil, this is

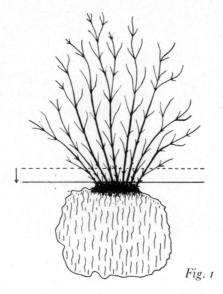

Fig. 1

no disadvantage, because many roots will develop on these shoots and will benefit the growth of the plants. If the soil around the root ball is then pressed firm, the plants will be sure to take.

32

Calluna vulgaris 'H. E. Beale'

Calluna vulgaris 'Boskoop'

una vulgaris 'Golden Rivulet'

Calluna vulgaris 'Darkness'

una vulgaris 'Mullion'

Calluna vulgaris 'Barnett Anley'

2 A heather garden in the Drenthe district

Bungalow with a heather garden

Watering

In a dry period, particularly soon after planting, the heather garden may need to be watered. In theory, wait as long as possible before watering, because once you have started you are recommended to continue until it rains again, as it tends to bring the feeding roots nearer the surface, especially if only light sprinkling has been given. This applies to all types of soil, but sandy soil in particular can dry out again very rapidly. If the mains water comes from a chalky area, it is safer to use rain water on summer-flowering heathers.

Watering with a can, with or without a rose, is time-consuming, and frequently not enough water is given by this method. So it is better to use a hose, either held in the hand or laid down between the plants. Hoses equipped with a sprinkler head – of which there are many different sizes and types – can also be used. Take care that puddles do not form.

The best time for watering is in the evening. The water can then soak in deeply enough during the night to reach the lower roots and less will be evaporated from the surface.

A further point to remember is that, even though the soil may be wet enough, the plants can be kept in better condition by giving a light sprinkling now and then; it keeps the foliage fresh by washing off dust and other pollutants.

Pruning

There are all sorts of opinions about the pruning of heathers. The way of least resistance is the view taken by A. T. Johnson in *Hardy Heaths* (1956): 'Nothing in the nature of regular shearing or clipping should be attempted . . . Personally, I much prefer to see the shrubs growing in their own natural manner, and very rarely prune any of them.' Pruning can also be omitted to save labour, and when necessary the heathers replaced by new plants.

· My own view, however, is that to keep heathers in good condition it is better to prune the plants carefully every year: I would say that it is undoubtedly one of the most important operations. However strange it may sound, when Ericas and Callunas are cultivated their growth must be controlled to a certain extent by man. People sometimes remark: 'The heathers in my garden are now four or five years old; they have grown very tall, flower badly and are getting straggly.' Then will often follow the question: 'What can I do about it?' In such a garden, where the plants have apparently never been pruned, nothing much can be done. Old *Calluna* plants in particular, that have not been pruned for years or possibly never, do not send out new shoots readily or may not even shoot at all when they are cut back hard to the old wood. In fact, one can only recommend digging them up and starting again with young ones.

Callunas, Daboecias and Ericas must all be pruned early on to make sure that the plants keep growing well. It does not make much difference in principle whether they are 2- or 3-

years old when planted; they must all be trimmed after planting. If planting is done in the autumn, wait until spring. Pruning stimulates good growth and stooling of the plants, so that in general they remain more compact. Annual pruning is particularly important for the foliage plants, such as *Calluna vulgaris* 'Gold Haze' and 'Sunset'. The better the young growth of these cultivars, the more beautifully coloured is the foliage in winter.

Under natural conditions often nothing happens for years on end to the heathers, and as a result the plants become tall and bare and flowering declines. To rejuvenate moors large areas of heather in Britain are burnt under controlled conditions – muirburn or swaling. This results in the development of new, free-flowering, young heather from the old roots and from seed. Here man is intervening to prevent the development of coarse leggy plants.

Wild animals, chiefly grouse, and domestic ones, notably sheep, also keep the heather on the moors short and consequently vigorous; and large areas are regularly cut in the British Isles for peat.

When to prune

The best time to prune summer-flowering heaths is between mid-March and mid-April, although it is sometimes done as early as October-November. But it has also been found that if plants with coloured young foliage, such as *Calluna vulgaris* 'Sally-Anne Proudley', 'Spring Cream', 'Spring Torch' and *Erica* × *watsonii* 'Dawn' are trimmed in the second half of August their shoot tips show up better in the spring.

Heathers that flower in winter or spring (*Erica carnea, E.* × *darleyensis* and *E. erigena*) must not be trimmed until after flowering. Flower buds are formed very soon after, so it is essential to do this immediately. Certain cultivars of winter-flowering heathers, however, have such a compact growth that it is difficult to trim them.

Heathers that have been planted in the autumn should not be pruned until the spring.

When heather is pruned, flowering will be delayed. In large areas with a single cultivar a difference in flowering time can be brought about by differential pruning (as regards time and method).

How to prune

The way in which heather should be pruned depends to a great extent on the species and cultivar. For a keen gardener who grows a great range of varieties it is considerably more complicated than in a normal garden.

It is obvious that heathers with a tall lax habit must be cut back harder than the dwarfs. *Calluna* cultivars such as, for instance, the vigorous, erect-growing 'Long White' and a number of forms of *Erica vagans* may be pruned back hard. Low-growing varieties of *Calluna*, such as 'Alba Plena' and 'County Wicklow', should be pruned proportionately, whereas the trimming of the dwarf forms such as 'Foxii Nana' can be limited to clipping away the rather longer sprigs carrying the old flowering spikes. This also applies to a variety like the prostrate 'Mrs. Ronald Gray'. Really these dwarf forms require little or no pruning.

The winter-flowering types, particularly the *Erica carnea* cultivars, on the whole require less pruning. With *Daboecia* it is mainly a matter of removing the old flowering shoots.

It is advisable to prune plants unevenly. If you prune too hard, the plants become separate rounded clumps which do not meet and cover the whole surface of the ground. Moreover, plants that have been shorn heavily into rounded clumps look unnatural (see Fig. 2).

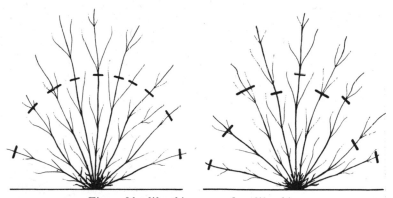

Fig. 2 Not like this . . . but like this

When the plants cover the ground closely a micro-climate develops favourable to their growth. If the sun beats down too fiercely on the soil and on the shallow root systems around the plants, this will sometimes lead to root scorching. And close cover keeps the weeds down.

For most gardeners secateurs are the best and most convenient tool for pruning, provided they fit the hand well. There are several sizes and types on the market. Small ones are more comfortable to hold even in a large hand and clipping is therefore easier than with those that are too large to be grasped easily. These are tiring to work with and reduce efficiency.

A pruning knife requires a certain amount of manual dexterity, while with shears the heather is often shorn too smooth, so that the plant does not show to full advantage. Skilful pruners, however, manage to avoid pruning too close with shears.

Protection

In Continental countries such as Holland and Germany many heathers need protecting with branches of fir or the like during the winter months. In the British Isles, this is never done. Some species, such as *Erica ciliaris* and *E. erigena*, and most tree heaths, will not stand the winter cold of areas like central Scotland, or adverse microclimates such as frost pockets. Certain cultivars, chiefly from warmer climes, may suffer. For example the true, and scarce, *Calluna* 'Elegantissima Walter Ingwersen' from Portugal must be overwintered in a cold house; *E. ciliaris* 'Maweana', of Portuguese origin too, and *E.* × *darleyensis* 'Arthur Johnson' are sometimes susceptible. *E. erigena* 'W. T. Rackliff' can lose stems. Soil heaving can also cause trouble with young plants in times of frost.

But the fact is that the great majority of forms of European heathers are hardy, and winter weather is no problem. The best insurance against loss from any cause is always to have young plants coming on from cuttings.

Pests and diseases

One of the great advantages of growing heathers is that there is rarely trouble from pests or disease. Of course, as in natural heathland, trouble can occur. But usually the damage caused to heather by insects is trifling compared with that caused to many other sorts of plant. With a single exception, this also applies to diseases. All plants are perhaps specially susceptible during the artificial conditions of propagation, from the time of taking the cuttings until the plants are ready for putting out.

At the present time, when so much is being talked about the conservation of nature, and quite rightly so, it is not easy to write about diseases and pests that can virtually only be controlled by chemicals. It is especially difficult in a book like this, written mainly for the very many gardeners who are gradually coming to care about their environment. We cannot avoid mentioning some, but will try to limit the use of chemicals to cases where they are absolutely necessary.

Control by chemicals can sometimes prove difficult for the keen amateur, because he may not use all those that a professional grower can. Chemicals for ordinary use are put on the market in small packages at garden centres, seed merchants, florists and such-like suppliers. Always read carefully the instructions and warnings on the label.

Before reaching for a chemical, it is as well first to have a look at the cultural conditions. If the water supply, the pH and the nutrient status of the soil are not good, the plants will grow poorly or may show abnormalities. Unthrifty plants are always more likely to be attacked by disease.

The symptoms and possible control measures for diseases and pests of *Calluna* and *Erica* will now be described, should trouble arise.

Pests

The heather beetle (Lochmaea suturalis)

The heather beetle is hardly ever found (in the British Isles), except on moors where it is sporadic in its outbreaks. The larvae and beetles destroy the terminal buds and young leaves, as a result of which the shoots die off. The larvae start feeding at the end of May. Initially they are pale green but later on greyish brown. The young beetles appear in August and September. They are about 6 mm long and olive brown in colour with a black head.

The best control is to cut back the plants. Ordinary gardeners cannot buy the chemicals that control beetles commercially.

Red spider (Tetranychus species)

These very small mites form a cocoon from a tissue of threads mainly on the lower surface of the leaves, and suck sap from the leaves. They are scarcely visible to the naked eye, but the web can often be seen. The leaves turn a rusty colour and later on whole shoots turn brown. The pest is most likely to spread in dry, warm weather in late summer. But it affects heathers less than many other plants.

There are various chemicals on the market suitable for the control of red spider and certain insects (aphids, for example); some are in aerosols. Most of these are poisonous to bees, so it is better not to use them at flowering time.

Diseases

Hygiene and healthy plants will ensure that few, if any, ever get diseased. Diseases that might occur are:

Wilt disease or root rot (Phytophthora cinnamomi)

This has given trouble in some parts in recent years. It is a soil fungus that occurs mainly in wet places, because moisture is essential for its spread. Plants become infected through the roots when the soil is moist and the temperature high enough, as can happen in the months of June to September. Rapid spread of the infection tends to occur after a very warm period followed within a few days by a great deal of rain.

The symptoms appear about a month later. The leaves of the attacked plants, or of a few shoots, turn an ashen green. On *Calluna* the base of the shoots frequently becomes a reddish brown. The tips of the shoots droop and within a few weeks the plants are dead. In cool, damp weather the process is slower. The root systems of diseased plants become wholly or partially brown and rotten. The fungus forms thick-walled resting spores that can survive in the soil for many years. The disease can at present be controlled most effectively by steaming the soil or by disinfecting it with chemicals. But there are several drawbacks to this. Soil disinfection may usually only be done by licensed operators. Moreover, after soil disinfection one has to allow a long interval before the ground can be planted up again.

Research has shown that the fungus can be killed in the soil by low temperatures. If the soil temperature in winter – presumably for a period of several weeks – is low enough, and the frost can penetrate the ground deeply enough, infection by this fungus is highly unlikely. A hard winter is thus good for the control or suppression of the disease.

In gardens the best method is to dig up the suspect plants as soon as possible and to replace the infected soil with fresh. When doing this, make sure that infected soil does not fall on other parts of the garden! Diseased plants must always be quickly burnt. A more recent practice is to cut down diseased plants to ground level and burn them thus leaving the soil undisturbed. It is difficult to know how far the fungus has spread in the soil.

It is important to practise garden hygiene right from the very beginning. Cuttings should only be taken from completely healthy plants, and the planting of suspect material on disinfected soil is highly undesirable.

Thread mould (Rhizoctonia solani)

Cuttings are most commonly attacked by this fungus. The stem turns blackish brown at soil level. The roots can also be attacked, but not so severely as by *Phytophthora*. In many cases you can see with the naked eye, but even better with a magnifying glass, fungal threads as fine as cobwebs on the soil and on the infected plants. The fungus persists in the soil. It, too, can spread rapidly under conditions of high temperature and plenty of moisture. Plants are more susceptible if the growing conditions are unsatisfactory.

An attack can be checked by reducing the temperature and by keeping the top layer of soil as dry as possible. Various chemicals, for example those containing captan and maneb, are available. They should be sprayed at the rate of 3 g per litre of water every two weeks from June onwards. Infected plants or parts of plants must first be carefully removed. By regularly examining cuttings for infection, the disease will be discovered at an early stage so that it can be controlled easily.

Grey mould (Botrytis cinerea)

This fungus occurs mainly on dead plant tissues, but in certain conditions it can also attack healthy young plants. A thick, mouse-grey mould appears that, unlike thread mould, forms spores. The cuttings rot and die off.

To control, this any infected parts must be removed. In greenhouses and frames be careful to keep the air dry by ventilating as much as possible. To prevent an attack, spray or, better still, dust with one of the various compounds, for example those based on thiram (= TMTD). This treatment must be repeated regularly.

Other Diseases

Occasionally a few other, less important diseases can occur. In greenhouses mildew *(Oidium ericinum)* sometimes develops, when a white mealy coating forms over the leaves and stems. The leaves turn brown and fall off from the bottom of the shoot upwards.

The leaves can also fall prematurely as a result of rust attack *(Uredo ericae)*, when orange-yellow, dusty spore masses can be seen on the leaves.

Honey fungus *(Armillariella (Armillaria) mellea)* is a soil fungus that can attack nearly any plant. It would be wise, however, when making a garden, to remove old tree stumps, because if they happened to be infected with the honey fungus the infection could spread.

Heather rhizomorph fungus or dieback *(Marasmius androsaceus)* may occur, mainly on older shoots of *Calluna*, as a result of which they die or even the whole plant dies. With both *Armillariella* and *Marasmius* rhizomorphs can be seen around the stem and among the roots. These are thread-like structures of tissue by means of which the fungus spreads through the soil. In *Armillariella* these are browny black and are sometimes as

43

thick as a bootlace, while those of *Marasmius* resemble horse-hair.

In recent years a brown discolouration of the growing tips has quite often been observed on *Calluna*. Sometimes the whole plant dies. Unlike wilt disease *(Phytophthora)* in which even the roots rot, this attack is not always fatal. The damage can be limited by cutting off the brown tips. For a long time the cause of this disease was not known. It is now supposed that in many cases the brown discolouration is caused by the leaf eelworm *(Aphelenchoides ritzemabosi)*. Sometimes the plants may show the symptoms, but one cannot actually diagnose an attack by this parasite.

Should any of these rare ailments occur, guidance on their treatment can be found in a general manual or from a horticultural establishment.

Weeds

Weeds can grow in heather gardens too! First of all it should be said that if they can be got rid of mechanically (by weeding, hoeing or scuffling), you should not resort to chemicals. It is true that many weedkillers are much less poisonous than most compounds used against pests or diseases, but when you use weedkillers you are interfering with the environment. Unless it is absolutely necessary, you should, as with pests and diseases, not spray at all or at least do so as little as possible. A heather garden can be regularly hand weeded. If it is scuffled with a Dutch hoe it may look well cared for and tidy, but many of the fine roots just below the surface are liable to be damaged, and this means that the heathers grow less quickly and heather seedlings too are destroyed. In contrast, even a light covering of moss may not be unwelcome as a form of ground cover. The soil will be firmer, but this is no disadvantage to heathers. Until the heathers cover the ground, a soil that is carpeted with mosses and algae and with seedlings of *Calluna* and *Erica* is a pleasant sight. Moreover, it is fairly well protected against too strong sunshine.

If you spray regularly to control weeds, then naturally the mosses and the heather seedlings will be killed too – but of course the latter must be kept under control too.

Control

If the area to be treated is large, or for other compelling reasons chemical control has to be used, you can spray on soils

45

with at least 3% organic matter in March-April (after pruning the heathers) with simazine (Gesatop-50) at 15 g per 100 m² in 10 to 20 litres of water. Granular simazine (Gesatop-G), with 2% active ingredient, may also be applied at the rate of 400 g per 100 m², possibly mixed with sand to obtain a more even distribution. For peaty soils with more than 20% organic matter, twice the quantity of simazine is recommended.

Before either herbicide is applied the soil should be really moist, and they are most effective when followed by a heavy shower. For the next four to six weeks the soil must not be disturbed.

Not all types of weeds are equally sensitive; Sheep's Sorrel *(Rumex acetosella)* especially is very persistent. This, and all other perennial weeds such as Couch-grass, should have been removed before any planting was undertaken; and any of their seedlings which subsequently appear, must be promptly dealt with.

Intensive research has shown that the breakdown of simazine in the soil is good to very good. The more organic matter there is present in the soil, the more rapidly does this compound disappear. Simazine is broken down in the soil mainly by micro-organisms but the breakdown is also affected by temperature and moisture.

Simazine is not toxic, or only very slightly so, to the soil fauna. It does not attack rubber or metals and does not irritate the skin.

There are other herbicides available, for example those which kill all the weeds on open patches, but in view of their limited applications in heather gardens, we need not go into these any further.

Labelling

There will undoubtedly be many gardeners who get intense pleasure from their plants without knowing their names. A garden is no less beautiful for this; the flowering is as good and ultimately that's what it is all about.

Fortunately there are also many people who like having their plants named. They will talk to other people about their garden and their experiences, and when doing this call the plants by their names. Moreover, reliable labelling and correct naming of the plants often comes in useful, especially when cutting material is being distributed. Propagators, in particular, can reproduce material on an extensive scale, so correct naming and labelling are important. In this way one can make sure that the customer gets what he asks for, which he is surely entitled to.

For those who want to have their plants well and permanently named, I will mention here a few simple ways of labelling.

How to label

There are all sorts of plastic labels on the market for hanging on the plant or for sticking in the ground, which can be easily written on with a good garden pencil. The plastic does not decompose, and since the label is soon shaded by the plant it remains legible for several years. (**Fig** 3a.)

Writing on the labels with a felt pen is not to be recommended. The letters usually fade very quickly, particularly in direct sunlight.

You can also buy aluminium labels which you can write on with a lead pencil and the writing will remain legible for years (see Fig. 3b). The label can be readily found when wanted if it is placed, for instance, on or in the most southerly plant of a group.

Some people prefer a label that stands well above the plants or in front of them, on which the name can be read clearly. This can be done, for instance, by punching the names on self-adhesive plastic strips and sticking these on to labels about 30 cm long (see Fig. 4).

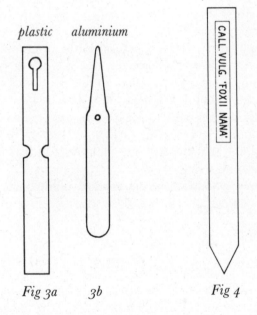

plastic   *aluminium*

CALL.VULG. 'FOXII NANA'

Fig 3a   *3b*   *Fig 4*

If you find these labels too prominent – as many do – it is better to name the plants by the methods described first. You can also draw a plan, to show the positions of the various plants. Such a plan is desirable anyway, because it often happens that for one reason or another a label gets lost.

48

3 An English heather garden with broad grass paths

Back garden with heather and other plants

4 *Erica carnea* 'Springwood White'

Erica carnea 'Praecox Rubra'

Erica cinerea 'Atrorubens'

Erica cinerea 'Golden Hue'

Erica cinerea 'Alba Minor '

Erica cinerea 'C. D. Eason'

Propagation

Heathers are nowadays propagated almost entirely by cuttings. Not so long ago they were multiplied mainly by layering and division and this method is still occasionally practised today. Propagation by seed is practical only if large areas are to be planted entirely with forms of wild species. The cultivated varieties must be propagated vegetatively in order to preserve the characters for which they were selected. With seed, these characters are normally lost.

Layering

Layering and division is a method of propagation particularly suitable for the amateur. The process is as follows. Some healthy, well developed plants are put in a bed enriched with peat and woodland soil. The plants are set slightly deeper in the ground than usual. The shoots are bent from the centre of the plant outwards so as to form a ring. Some soil is placed within this ring and a stone is laid on top of it – the stone is there to press the shoots down slightly and, even more important, to keep the soil moist. If it dries out, root formation will be severely checked.

In the spring following the layering, the earthed-up plants can be lifted and divided into 5 to 10 parts, as required, each with a number of roots. In this way from a single plant an amateur can obtain several plants within a year, with which he can enrich his garden (see Fig. 5). If cuttings were made

49

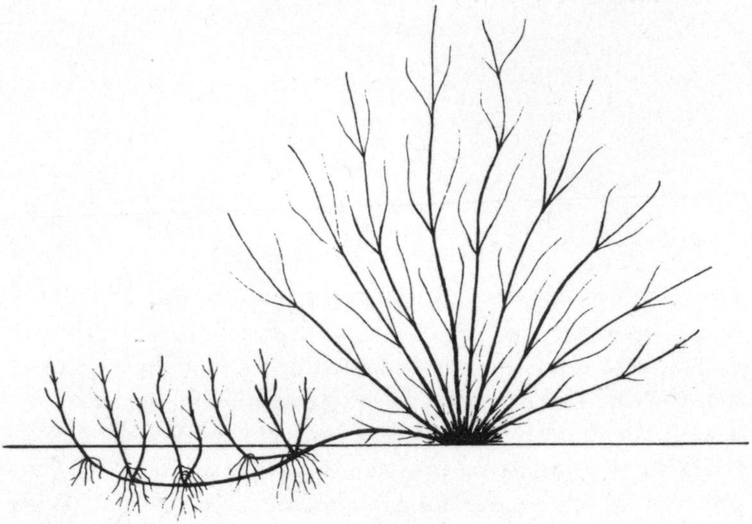

Fig. 5

from the same plant it would take at least a year longer before
a good plant was produced. An amateur must therefore consider carefully what he wants before he starts to propagate
heathers.

Cuttings

Taking cuttings is a method of propagation that is generally
very successful, particularly if a large number of plants have to
be raised. With this too you must, of course, start with healthy
plants.

Cuttings can be rooted in various places, for instance in a
cold frame under (single) Dutch lights, under double glass (see
Fig. 6) in a cold frame or greenhouse, in a heated greenhouse
under a glass cover or in a heated greenhouse under mist. This
last method is used mainly by nurserymen who want to root a

50

great many cuttings rapidly. Bottom heat of $5°$–$6°C$. above air temperature is always a help.

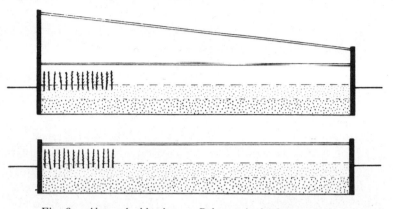

Fig. 6   Above: double glass.   Below: single glass..

The propagating frame

The ideal situation for a propagating frame is in a draught-free, north-facing position, provided that surrounding trees and buildings do not keep away too much light. A frame may also be sited in other positions, but then it must be well shaded in sunny weather. This is difficult to do if one cannot be watching it all day. If necessary, the lights of the frame can be sprayed or painted with whitewash and/or shaded with a mat with narrow slats that can be rolled up (a so-called roller blind). In very sunny weather a double blind must be laid over the frame.

Another method of shading that is very effective is the following: boards with notches in them are set edgewise in the frame and slats are inserted in the notches so that the sun's rays do not fall directly into the frame (see Fig. 7).

The soil in the frame must be well drained. If it is not, a layer 10 to 20 cm deep of pebbles, cinders, flowerpot crocks or

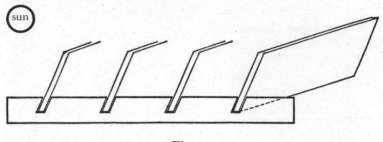

Fig. 7.

coarse sand must be placed at the bottom. On top of this can be laid the rooting medium (i.e. the cutting compost) to a depth of 5 to 6 cm, and the cuttings can be inserted into this. They may also quite easily be inserted into pots or boxes 5–8 cm high. The advantage of this is that the frame has to be open for only a short time while the pots or boxes are being put into it. A disadvantage of inserting the cuttings directly into the cold frame is that the lights remain off for too long while the cuttings are being set, so that the sun and wind can do their worst. An advantage is that the cuttings that have been inserted directly in the frame are in less danger of drying out than those in pots or boxes.

The level of the cutting compost in the frame, or of the soil on which the pots or boxes are placed, should be the same as, or higher than, the level outside the frame. This is to prevent waterlogging of the compost during the winter. It is important that the air and moisture conditions in the frame should not be subject to too great fluctuations, especially while the cuttings are rooting.

The cutting compost

Opinions about cutting composts or rooting media vary very widely. Very often 4 parts peat and 1 part sand (free of lime and salts) by volume are used. Some people prefer half and half, while in nurseries cuttings are almost always inserted in 100% peat. If necessary the peat should be put through a sieve and moistened so that it is just less than saturated. This means that when a handful of the compost is squeezed no water runs out.

The sand ensures good drainage and aeration, and it also has an effect on the pH (degree of acidity). The more sand that is mixed with the compost, the higher the pH is likely to be. If a great deal of sand is used in the cutting compost it can even make the pH too high. When it is ready for use, it is put into well cleaned pots or boxes and pressed in evenly and fairly firmly (but not too firmly). The corners should not be overlooked. There should be some holes in the bottom so that any excess water can run out. The surface can be smoothed with a small slat of wood and covered with a thin (2–3 mm) layer of sand to prevent the growth of algae.

When to take cuttings

The right time to take cuttings depends on the ripeness of the material. The type of soil in which the plants are growing has an effect on this. Cutting material on plants grown in sandy soil is ripe sooner than that on those in peat soil. It must not be too hard, but on the other hand not too soft or too limp. One learns by experience.

You can start to take cuttings of *Erica carnea* as early as the middle of June, just before flower initiation, when the shoot tips are nearly fully grown. If cuttings are taken later it is advisable to cut off the flower buds, although this is being done less and less. It is important not to take the cuttings too late; *E. carnea* becomes woody very quickly and this impedes root formation.

All other Ericas and Callunas, and many other ericaceous plants, can be propagated in August or September. In theory, cuttings can be taken when the material is sufficiently well

53

ripened, but August is usually best for rooting cuttings in a cold frame. They will then be well rooted before the winter sets in, which is a very important factor in overwintering. Those that have not yet rooted can easily dry out during the winter.

If a heated greenhouse is available, so-called tip cuttings may be taken even as late as October-November. These are the tips above the part of the shoot that has flowered. Certain cultivars of *Calluna vulgaris*, for instance the late-flowering 'Hibernica', can also be successfully rooted in March or April.

Preparing the cuttings

The ways in which cuttings may be made differ slightly.

Side shoots can be pulled off and used just as they are, with no further treatment. By pulling the shoots off one leaves a so-called heel at the base that does not need to be cut off. This method is little used in Holland; the base of the cuttings is nearly always cut with a sharp knife as horizontally as possible (see Fig. 8).

If side shoots are not available, the tip portion and the portion below the flowers (lowest portion) may be used (see Fig. 9).

The tips to be used must often be allowed to grow on once

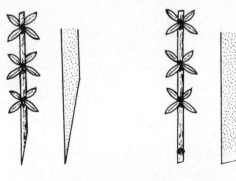

Fig. 8   Not like this...   but like this.

flowering is over. This material is usually too soft for early propagation and you may have to wait until November before taking cuttings from it. Then, of course, it must be rooted in a greenhouse.

If you want to propagate earlier than this – when the plants have already formed flower buds but tip cuttings have not yet developed – cuttings may be taken from the portion of the shoot below the flower buds provided it has not become too woody. Cuttings from this lowest portion of the shoot are often too hard, particularly if they are taken too late (in October or November).

If, when the cuttings are taken, their tips are not yet hard enough, they can be cut out or pinched out (see Fig. 10). This encourages the cuttings to branch at an early age, which improves the development of the young plants.

Shoots of more than a year old often root poorly or do not root at all. It is therefore undesirable to take cuttings from them.

The length of the cuttings depends to a great extent on the species and cultivar. Usually it is 4 to 6 cm. Recently, however, people have been tending more and more to use cuttings 2 to 4 cm long. New cultivars are even cut into pieces 1 to 2 cm long. The fact that the growth of the young plants is sometimes poor in the first year is often the result of having used too small cuttings. With tree heaths, cuttings 6 to 10 cm long may well be taken.

It is advisable, although not absolutely necessary, to remove the leaves from the bottom third of the cutting (see Fig. 11). This can be done easily and quickly by stripping them off with the thumb and forefinger.

Fig. 9   a. tip portion;   b. lowest portion.

55

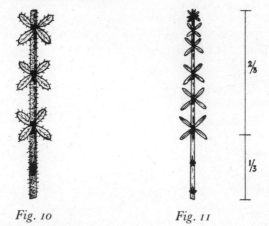

Fig. 10   Fig. 11

Inserting the cuttings

The prepared cuttings should be inserted in the rooting medium as quickly as possible. The depth of insertion depends on the length of the cutting. In general it can be said: the shallower the planting, the better it is for rooting. If the cutting does not fall over, it is in theory deep enough for rooting. Generally this means inserting a quarter (!) of the cutting (see Fig. 12).

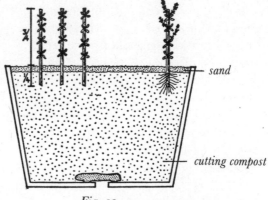

Fig. 12

If the cuttings are not firm enough to insert easily, small holes can be pricked in the cutting compost before insertion. Some nurserymen and amateurs use a small slat of wood with nails in it, pressing it into the medium before planting the cuttings (see Fig. 13).

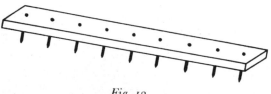

Fig. 13

The distance apart at which the cuttings should be set depends to some extent on the species or cultivar. A distance of about 1½ cm is quite usual. Planting too close leads to difficulties in separating the cuttings when they are being lifted in spring, especially if they are well rooted.

Before the boxes or pots of cuttings are placed in the frame, they should be well moistened with a mist sprayer or, better still, a watering can with a fine rose. The space between the cuttings and the glass should be kept as small as possible. A space of 1 to 2 cm is quite enough.

In a heated greenhouse you must be careful that the temperature does not rise too high – possibly as a result of soil warming. Some species are very sensitive to high temperatures. For example, *Erica carnea* can tolerate a high soil temperature much less well than the hybrid *E.* × *darleyensis*.

Growth substances

Growth substances like Seradix, which are used for cuttings of very many woody plants in the nursery, are normally unnecessary for heathers. *Rhododendron* hybrids, on the other hand, are always treated with growth substances to obtain better and more rapid rooting.

57

If heathers are propagated at any time other than the proper season, when the material is usually too hard, it may be advisable to use a weak growth substance such as Seradix 1. In general, one needs a wide experience in the use of growth substances to obtain good rooting with them.

Time needed for rooting

Rooting is affected by many different factors. The time needed depends in the first place on the species and cultivar and then on the temperature, by day and at night. When the cuttings start to grow, this is usually a sign that root formation is also proceeding. By gently pulling the tips of the cuttings, you can feel whether this is so. But remember, the first tiny roots are very delicate!

Calluna vulgaris, Erica ciliaris, E. tetralix and *Daboecia cantabrica* on the whole root easily and quickly. Slightly less satisfactory are *E. carnea, E.* × *darleyensis, E. cinerea* and particularly *E. vagans* and *E. terminalis.* One must reckon on a minimum of four weeks and a maximum of eight to ten weeks before the cuttings are well rooted. In a heated greenhouse under mist the cuttings sometimes begin to root after only one week.

The results vary greatly from year to year. What is good for one cultivar can be much less successful with another. One thing is certain: practice makes perfect.

Further treatment

During the autumn, winter and spring you must inspect the rooted cuttings regularly to see that they are moist enough. Too much moisture, however, is fatal; it can encourage the development of grey and thread moulds. Diseased parts of plants and/or cuttings that have died off completely are best removed as soon as possible.

For the first five to eight days the frame should be kept shut

58

and shaded. After that ventilate regularly, opening the frame for 5 to 10 minutes two or three times a week. By opening the frame always at the higher side, the condensation water runs off to the lower side of the frame. This area can therefore become excessively wet. Watch out for this!

If a frame is situated with the lights sloping to the south, take care that the cuttings along the higher side of the frame are kept moist enough. The reflection from the wall of the frame tends to make the cuttings dry out more quickly here.

The glass can be taken off the frame during dull or rainy weather to harden off the young plants (rooted cuttings) still further. When night frosts occur, they should be covered up again. The spring sunshine will soon make the young plants take on a brighter, more natural colour.

Growing on the plants

When the rooted cuttings have been sufficiently well hardened off, they may be planted out in a nursery bed at the end of April or beginning of May. The little plants must be separated very carefully, and special care must be taken not to allow the roots to dry out.

Woodland soil and/or peat should be added to the nursery bed; this makes a well aerated mixture. Naturally it must also be well moistened.

The spacing at which the rooted cuttings should be planted out depends on the species and cultivar. That generally used varies from 6 to 10 cm, with the plants being set alternately in adjacent rows. This will only be enough for one growing season. It is advisable in the following spring to set out the plants again at a wider spacing or to plant them out directly in the garden.

Once the material has been planted out it does not need to be protected from the sun, provided it is well hardened. During warm, drying weather water the beds well and regularly.

Instead of putting the young plants in beds, they may be potted up. Plastic pots of 5 to 7 cm are suitable, as well as earthenware (clay) pots. Peat pots (for example, Jiffy pots) that will decompose have also been used with much success. When plastic pots are used special attention must be paid to watering, because the amount of water available in them is limited.

The potting soil must be of good quality. Nowadays there are various ready-to-use composts available in the shops. Almost any good flower-grower's soil is suitable for ericaceous plants, because these all have a peat basis. A specific potting soil for them is a mixture of 70% peat and 30% decomposed pine needle litter. The pots must be plunged. The rim of the pot should be just below the soil surface. In other respects the treatment of potted plants is the same as that of plants set out in nursery beds. An advantage of plants grown in pots is that, when they are planted out, they continue to grow better because the roots are hardly disturbed at all.

Systematics and naming

Before discussing the range of the species and cultivars of heathers, it would perhaps be helpful if I first dealt with a number of expressions and technical terms. The classification of the plant kingdom and nomenclature (the naming of plants) are somewhat indigestible subjects for most gardeners.

Certain commonly occurring terms are regularly misused. One frequently hears the question: 'What is a cultivar?' or 'What is a genus?' The ordinary gardener is often not well informed about such expressions as 'clone' and 'sport', and many do not realise that these terms are of importance, if they want to improve their knowledge of plants by studying the literature, because they are generally used without any further explanation.

In order to help the reader to understand some of these subjects, definitions or schematic outlines will be given, each time with one or more examples. More details can, of course, be found about these matters in technical works.

At the end of the book is a glossary in which some technical terms are explained, and the meanings are given of a number of scientific epithets.

Classification of the plant kingdom

Like the animal kingdom, the plant kingdom is arranged in a definite order (divisions, sub-divisions etc.). The classification, (and various systems exist) is based mainly on morphological and anatomical* characters, but also on the method of reproduction. The International Codes of Nomenclature recognise certain categories for grouping similar plants. The main higher ranks, with just two examples each of their constituents (Names covering the heathers are in **bold** type,) include:

DIVISION: **Spermatophyta (Magnoliophyta)** (seed plants). Pteridophyta (ferns).

SUBDIVISION: **Angiospermae** (flowering plants). Gymnocarpae (Pinacae) (conifers).

CLASS: **Dicotyledones** (with two seed leaves). Monocotyledones (with one).

ORDER: **Ericales** (Heaths, Wintergreens, Crowberries etc.) Primulales (Primroses etc.)

FAMILY: **Ericaceae.** Pyrolaceae (Wintergreens).

The subfamilies of the Ericaceae, with their genera mentioned in this book, are

ERICOIDEAE: *Bruckenthalia. Calluna. Erica.*

ARBUTOIDEAE: *Andromeda. Arbutus. Arctostaphylos. Arctous. Cassiope. Chamaedaphne. Enkianthus. Epigaea. Gaulnettya. Gaultheria. Leucothoë. Lyonia. Oxydendrum. Pernettya. Pieris. Zenobia.*

RHODODENDROIDEAE: *Daboecia. Kalmia. Ledum. Leiophyllum. Loiseleuria. Menziesia. Phyllodoce. Rhododendron* (incl. *Azalea*). *Rhodothamnus. Tripetaleia.*

VACCINOIDEAE: *Gaylussacia. Vaccinium.*

* morphology = external structure; anatomy = internal structure

Genera are made up of one or more species ('sp.', plural 'spp.'). *Calluna* is considered to have only one species, and so is a monotypic genus. *Erica* has well over 600, nearly all South African and generally tender in our islands, as well as numerous hybrids.

The main subdivisions of species are subspecies ('ssp.'), varieties ('var.') and forms ('f.'). *Erica azorica*, the Besom Heath in the Azores is now called *E. scoparia* ssp. *azorica*, and that in the Canaries ssp *platycodon* (and no doubt that in Madeira should be similarly distinguished). This indicates that they are geographical races of the typical Mediterranean *E. scoparia* ssp. *scoparia* (typical categories nowadays have to repeat the name of the category above them). *Calluna vulgaris* (which is normally called just *Calluna*) is typically hairless, i.e. the type specimen is hairless. So this is var. *vulgaris* (earlier *genuina* or *glabra*). But plants may be found with every degree of hairiness up to the close grey pubescence of, for example, 'Silver Queen'. These come under var. *hirsuta (ciliaris, incana, pilosa, pubescens, tomentosa)*, but just how much hairy covering is required for this variety is a matter of opinion (which is partly reflected in the various alternative names). The full classification of 'Silver Queen' is:

DIVISION:	Spermatophyta (Magnoliophyta)
SUBDIVISION:	Angiospermae
CLASS:	Dicotyledones
SUBCLASS:	Sympetalae (Metachlamydeae)
ORDER:	Ericales
FAMILY:	Ericaceae
SUBFAMILY:	Ericoideae
GENUS:	*Calluna*
SPECIES:	*vulgaris*
VARIETY:	*hirsuta*
CULTIVAR:	'Silver Queen'

Normally only the botanical categories of genus and below are set out in italics. The final category is horticultural: all the others are botanical and cover natural populations in the wild, from which all garden plants ultimately derive.

The nomenclatural rules for man-selected forms were first laid down in the International Code for 'Cultivated Plants in 1953. Before then garden varieties were often given names in Latin like wild plants. These have now to be amended to cultivar style, i.e. written in ordinary Roman type and not italics, and either prefaced with 'cv.' or put within single quotation marks, the latter now being generally preferred, each word in the name beginning with a capital letter. Thus what used to be written *alba rigida* must now be 'Alba Rigida'. What the eminent Dutchman Dr Beijerinck in his Monograph on the Scotch Heather called *Calluna vulgaris* var. *genuina* (*vulgaris* now) f. *praecox* subf. *tenuis* includes 'Tenuis' on which this category was based. All horticultural variants, as examples of natural variation, should fit into some botanical category as well.

All botanical categories and names are in Latin form; all new horticultural ones are now 'fancy', i.e. markedly different from Latin. But horticultural names in Latin form given before 1959 are to be retained unaffected, except for their being set out as cultivars, thus 'Alba Rigida' above.

Naming (nomenclature)

All known species of plants have scientific names in two parts: the system is now generally called binomial nomenclature. A species has a generic name (for example, *Calluna*) and a specific epithet (for example, *vulgaris*). The two words together are called the specific name. According to international agreement this scientific name is the only official one. It consists of words that, almost without exception, are Latin or words from another language (often Greek) that have been latinized.

Calluna vulgaris 'Silver Queen'

Calluna vulgaris 'Golden Haze'

lluna vulgaris 'Sally-Anne Proudley'

Calluna vulgaris 'Ralph Purnell'

lluna vulgaris 'Mrs. Ronald Grey'

Calluna vulgaris 'Golden Feather'

6 A heather garden with *Picea abies* 'Repens' and *Salix caprea pendula* 'Kilmarnock' (male form)

The use of a scientific name has the great advantage that anyone anywhere knows, or at least can find out, what was meant when this name is given. This is of the utmost importance both for science and for international trade which is expanding all the time.

Binomial nomenclature was introduced by the gifted Swedish botanist Carl von Linné, Linnaeus, (1707-1778), who developed this happy idea and first used it consistently in 1753 in his famous book *Species Plantarum* (The Species of Plants). Before that various different Latin names had arisen over the years for the same species. These ranged from a single word to phrases of 10 or more words.

Botanists and taxonomists after Linnaeus have continued to name and describe countless thousands of plants following his system, so his principles continue in use today.

Unfortunately the same plant has often been described under different names because it was not, or could not be, known, that it had been described and named already, or that the characters given to distinguish it from other species were unimportant, even illusory. This gave rise to synonyms, that is to say, more than one name for the same species.

Later on, international botanical congresses were held and various agreements made to obtain more unity in naming. Diverse views about nomenclature persisted, however, for a long time and were only settled in about 1930.

Following the Congress at Stockholm in 1950, there have been two internationally accepted Codes which control the naming of plants. They are the 'International Code of Botanical Nomenclature' and, based on it, the 'International Code of Nomenclature for Cultivated Plants'.

Since these naturally comprise many articles, we have summarized here in a simple form some of the most important rules and principles.

1. The principle of priority is followed; this means that of all the synonyms only the oldest valid one is recognised as correct.

In the case of the 'Higher Plants' (flowering plants and ferns), we do not go back further than the first edition of Linnaeus's *Species Plantarum* of 1753. Binomials published before this must be rejected.

2. If anyone gives a botanical name to a plant, he must, in order to do this validly, describe it 'officially', that is to say as fully as possible in Latin in a scientific journal or book.

3. Generic names must start with a capital letter, whereas it is now recommended that all specific epithets should start with a small one. One example is *Calluna vulgaris*; another is *Erica mackaiana*, even though this specific epithet commemorates J. T. Mackay (?1775–1862), and for that reason previously had been written with a capital initial. *Sabina officinalis* was later rechristened *Juniperus Sabina*; the specific epithet spelt with a capital initial because it is the old generic name, or the name all on its own, for the Savin. Nowadays it is recommended that this should be written as *Juniperus sabina* (with a small s), which makes it look like a false concord and hides the allusion to the ancient name; but it is more convenient, so the recommendation is almost universally followed. It has long been the rule among zoologists.

4. Whenever a species is transferred to another genus, the change of name follows fixed rules. Wherever possible the original specific epithet is kept. Thus Linnaeus called Ling *Erica vulgaris*. On the basis of morphological characters, Dr John Hull (1761–1843) in 1808 named and described it as *Calluna vulgaris*; the specific epithet was thus preserved.

Either name is equally valid and equally correct in its genus: it is just a matter of opinion whether the differences are sufficient to recognise two genera. In fact they very definitely are; but for covenience Ling is still often listed under *Erica* as *E. vulgaris*; and this is not wrong, merely not preferable.

As a result of research, many genera have been revised and their species distributed among a number of smaller genera. A good example of this is *Andromeda*. In addition to the typical

66

Andromeda (*A. polifolia* is a native), we now recognize the genera *Pieris, Leucothoë, Lyonia, Chamaedaphne, Zenobia* etc. Sometimes small genera are regrouped into the original 'large' genus.

Authors' names

Following the scientific name one may see the name of a person or, more commonly, an abbreviation of this. L. is the abbreviation for Linnaeus. He designated Ling *Erica vulgaris*; so, after the specific epithet *vulgaris* is placed his own name or the abbreviated Linn. or L., thus *Erica vulgaris* L. Dr. Hull transferred this species to *Calluna*, as was noted earlier, whence it is now cited as *Calluna vulgaris* (L.) Hull. By this is indicated that the specific epithet *(vulgaris)* was given by Linnaeus, and that Hull first produced the combination *Calluna vulgaris*. The bracketed (L.) should not be omitted, as sometimes happens. In addition to the very frequently occurring L., there are many thousands of authors' names – the author is the man who gave the plant the relevant name. Hort. following a plant name means '*hortorum*' (= of gardens). It is used mostly for names current among gardeners or nurserymen which have not been formally published.

Synonyms

A synonym (syn.) is a name used at one time but now deemed incorrect and superseded by the correct one, or it may be a correct one if the species is put in a different genus. A wrong name under which the plant is mistakenly known, may also be cited. A synonym may be added, in brackets, after the correct name. There can be synonyms of generic, specific, varietal or cultivar names. Examples are:
Pieris floribunda (syn. *Andromeda floribunda*); these are both correct names in their respective genera.

67

Erica terminalis (syn. *E. stricta*); the latter name was published after the former, so is incorrect under the principle of priority.
Calluna vulgaris var. *vulgaris* (syn. *C. vulgaris* var. *genuina*); it is now agreed that the typical variety of a species shall repeat the specific epithet.
Erica carnea 'Myretoun Ruby' (syn. 'Winter Jewel'); the former is the original name.
The 'syn.' may be omitted.

Popular names

In addition to the scientific names of plants, there are popular names, the names by which a plant is known in common speech in various countries and regions. Ling and Scotch heather are English names for *Calluna vulgaris*.

A plant may have many local names, not only in different countries (and languages) but also in the different parts of the same country: there may be several in use in a single area for the same plant. Thus, for instance, the daisy, which has the scientific name of *Bellis perennis* throughout the whole world, in Britain alone has some thirty different popular names, and other plants have more. Some local names are confusing because they duplicate the names of other plants; Bird's-eye, for instance, is used for numerous, usually blue-flowered, plants.

The daisy has other popular names elsewhere, but *Bellis perennis* is the correct scientific name anywhere. *Calluna vulgaris*, too, has only one correct scientific name in this genus, although in other languages it is called Struikheide (Dutch), Besenheide (German), Hedelyng (Danish), Bruyère commune (French), Brughiera (Italian), and Brezo (Spanish), to name only a few.

The above examples will make it plain what a babel can be avoided by the use of the correct scientific name.

Registration

The registration of the mass of the cultivated varieties of many plant genera and other groups is carried out by International Registration Authorities, officially recognised since 1955 – there are over 60 of them. All new garden plants should be reported to them. For the genera *Calluna, Daboecia* and *Erica*, this is the responsibility of the Heather Society. The work is carried out by Mr David McClintock. For a number of years close contact has been maintained with him on the subject of heather cultivars. Several registers are already published. A list of all the names used for hardy heathers will be found in Mr G. Yates' *Pocket Guide to Heather Gardening*, which appears in the bibliography.

Further notes on classification

Family

As the name implies, the genus *Erica* is the type genus of the Ericaceae, a large family. Most family names end in -aceae; there are eight exceptions, two of them are the Cruciferae (Crucifer family) and Gramineae (Grass family), but these are now also known as Brassicaceae and Pocaceae, after their type genera.

Genus

Linnaeus placed *Calluna* and *Daboecia* in the genus *Erica*. Later the plants called by him *Erica vulgaris* and *E. daboecii* were regrouped respectively, as *Calluna vulgaris* and, eventually, *Daboecia cantabrica*.

Species

A species is the basic unit in the classification of plants and animals. The word is often misused, for example where vari-

69

eties or cultivars are meant, as well as being muddled with specimens. Nurserymen often cannot cope with fine and changing details of classification and, for convenience, call all their plants species.

As has been mentioned earlier, the scientific name of a species consists of two words, i.e. the generic name and the specific epithet. *Calluna vulgaris* is such a biverbal name and represents a true species. So do *Erica tetralix, Andromeda polifolia* and *Vaccinium myrtillus*. Species are basically natural groupings of wild plants, even if some now survive only in cultivation.

A garden plant, for example *Erica tetralix* 'Helma', is not a species. It is a selected form that has been given the name 'Helma' and must be propagated vegetatively if its characters are to be preserved; so we call it a cultivated variety or cultivar (see p. 71). If this form of *Erica tetralix* (which was found in the wild in Holland) had been transferred to the garden and never given a name it would have been no more than an example of the natural range of variation in the species *E. tetralix*.

People may take different views whether a given plant should be considered a species, a subspecies or a variety. Sometimes a species is 'split' into two or more species, or two or more species may be 'lumped'. This is now often done on the grounds of anatomical characters, the number of chromosomes frequently being useful. Species come true from seed within their own limits of variation provided they have not been pollinated by another species.

Variety

The word 'variety' is much used in colloquial speech, but unfortunately often incorrectly. People often speak of a heather garden with many species and varieties, whereas they usually mean a few species and many cultivated varieties.

From a botanical point of view a variety is a slightly divergent natural group within a species. All plants may vary from seed. This is important as it enables them to compete with varying conditions. Wild populations of similar variants, often from differing habitats, may be singled out for naming as botanical varieties. The var. *pumilio* of *Pinus mugo* comes from the high mountains. It is always propagated by seed and varies slightly from plant to plant, but retains the dwarf stature imposed on it by its natural habitat.

Form

A form (f.) ranks lower than a variety (and a subform (subf.) even lower still). What it amounts to is that within a variety one or more forms may have been named, often on the basis of a single character such as, for instance, a different flower colour.

All white-flowered specimens of *Calluna* come under the collective appellation of *Calluna vulgaris* f. *alba*; or one could extend it to *Calluna vulgaris* var. *vulgaris* f. *alba*, if it were a hairless plant.

Cultivated variety

A cultivated variety or cultivar (cv. for short), is a distinct group of plants which, through the intervention of man, by whatever means, has been brought into cultivation and owes its name and existence to him. It may originally have arisen by selection from seedlings, by hybridization or by mutation. In order to maintain the characters for which it has been selected, for example flower colour, leaf size or growth, a perennial such as a heather must be propagated vegetatively (for instance, by cuttings) and so is a clone (see below). Clones will not normally come true from seed. When special strains of annuals do, they can become cultivars, but are never clones.

71

Clone

By the term 'clone' we mean a vegetatively propagated group of plants originating from a single individual. Thus all the specimens of *Erica tetralix* 'Helma' now in cultivation come from a single plant that was selected for its distinct characteristics among the common Cross-leaved Heaths growing in the wild. All the vegetatively propagated progeny of this plant will be exactly alike, even in the far-distant future, provided that no mutation arises.

Hybrid

Hybrids are plants that have arisen as a result of crossing two species, such as *Daboecia azorica* × *D. cantabrica*, now called *D.* × *scotica*. Selections from these, as from species, must be propagated vegetatively and then become cultivated varieties and get 'fancy' names.

Perhaps the best-known plant of this parentage is 'William Buchanan'. The correct way to cite this is *D.* × *scotica* 'William Buchanan', often shortened in practice to simple *Daboecia* 'William Buchanan'. This may however imply that the origin of the plant is uncertain. *Erica* 'Stuartii' was cited in this way until recognised as a mutant of *E.* × *praegeri*.

Mutation

A mutation, also called a sport, is a genetic change that has occurred suddenly usually in a portion of a plant, for instance a different flower colour, flower shape or growth. It is a natural phenomenon, but nowadays may also be induced, for example, by radiation.

When such an abnormal shoot is propagated, by cuttings, grafting or budding, the typical characters can be preserved and a new cultivar started. Very many plants have been obtained in this way and put on the market.

Calluna vulgaris 'Carmen' is a purple-red-flowered mutation of the purple 'Barnett Anley'. The other characters of the plant are virtually the same; only the flower colour is markedly different.

On the single white-flowered *Calluna vulgaris* 'Alba Elegans' there arose in Germany shortly before 1934 the double-flowered 'Alba Plena'. An abnormal shoot was found on this cultivar in England in 1951; it had golden foliage and, similarly, double white flowers. This was given the name 'Ruth Sparkes'.

An unfortunate tendency of a few mutations is that they are unstable and 'revert' to the original form. This can affect a portion of the plant, but may eventually affect all of it. Thus on the golden-leaved, double-flowered 'Ruth Sparkes' there may arise shoots with green leaves. If cuttings are taken from these shoots they remain like this, and we are left with none other than 'Alba Plena', whence 'Ruth Sparkes' originated. It can then even revert right back to the original 'Alba Elegans' with single flowers, whence 'Alba Plena' originated.

The cultivar 'Dart's Gold' was distributed in Holland in 1972, a further mutation of 'Ruth Sparkes' with a more compact habit of growth, but still with golden foliage which hardly reverts at all. A strange fact is that 'Dart's Gold' has normal 'single', not double flowers. In this case one could speak of a yellow-leaved 'Alba Elegans', whereas 'Ruth Sparkes' is a yellow 'Alba Plena'.

From the double-flowered 'Alba Plena' there arose not only the yellow-leaved 'Ruth Sparkes'; in England a sport of this was found in 1950 with mauve-pink double flowers. This was given the name 'Joan Sparkes'.

Reversion also occurs frequently in selections from *Daboecia cantabrica* 'Bicolor'. In order to preserve the two-coloured effect of the flowers you must take cuttings of shoots with both white and purple and/or purple-striped flowers. Propagation from shoots that bear only white or purple flowers is not advisable, because you hardly ever obtain bi-coloured flowers from these.

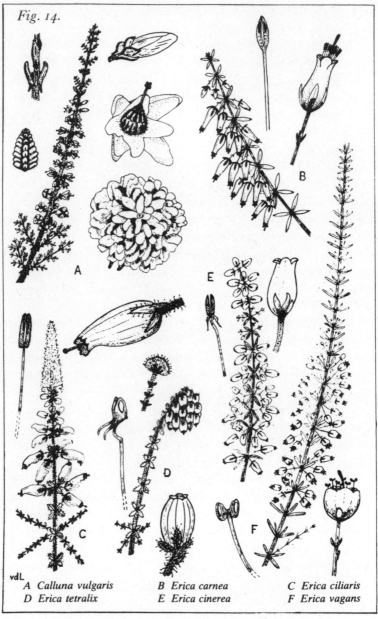

Fig. 14.

vdL
A Calluna vulgaris   B Erica carnea   C Erica ciliaris
D Erica tetralix   E Erica cinerea   F Erica vagans

Descriptions of the species and cultivars

The range of variation in Heathers

The most important characteristic of the cultivated Callunas and Ericas is the great variety of habit, leaf colour, flower colour, flowering time, etc. Thanks to the very different times of flowering, it is possible to have heathers in flower in the garden all the year round. Other merits, too, make *Calluna* and *Erica* useful for all sorts of purposes.

Callunas

An exceptionally wide range of variation can be observed among the cultivars of *Calluna vulgaris* alone. Thus some have markedly grey, hairy foliage (e.g. 'Silver Queen'), some yellow foliage in both winter and summer (e.g. 'Beoley Gold' and 'Christina'); others have bronzy-yellow foliage in the summer but turn to a magnificent orange or bright orange-red in autumn and winter (e.g. 'Fairy' and 'Robert Chapman'). The foliage of some, e.g. 'Durfordii', turns to blackish purple-brown in winter. In combination with bright green-leaved forms (e.g. 'French Grey'), a beautiful effect can be achieved with such plants, especially during the winter. There are also some with very prettily coloured young shoots, particularly in the spring (e.g. 'Mrs Pat' 'Sally-Anne Proudley', 'Spring Cream' and 'Spring Torch').

The flowers of Callunas are generally purple or purple-pink. There are also numerous white-flowered cultivars (about 130 have been named). A few cultivated forms are more pink (e.g. 'Hookstone' and 'Peter Sparkes'), while some others have purple-red flowers (e.g. 'Carmen' and 'Coccinea'). An exception is 'J. H. Hamilton'. This has pure salmon pink flowers, which are also double.

Over the years more than 40 double-flowered plants have been recorded. One of the oldest and best known is 'H. E. Beale'. Some others are 'Alba Plena', 'County Wicklow' and 'Tib'.

With the double-flowered Callunas, notably those like 'H. E. Beale', shoots can be cut in full bloom and inserted in damp moss, oasis or a cut potato; after that no more water need be given. The shoots dry out while the flower colour remains good for months. Double-flowered cultivars can also be stored, packed in plastic, in the freezing compartment of a refrigerator from September to, say, Christmas. The shoots must be thawed out gradually. If they are brought into a warm room too suddenly the flowers will discolour quickly.

Calluna cultivars differ greatly in flowering time. Some flower as early as about mid-June (e.g. 'Caerketton White' and 'Tenuis'), while 'Serlei' only starts to flower in September and 'Autumn Glow' waits until November or later.

They vary also in growth. In the wild, plants over 2 m high have been recorded, while along ditches and banks specimens have been found with shoots that hang down vertically *(Calluna vulgaris* f. *decumbens* subf. *pendula* e.g. 'Prostrata Flagelliformis'). Some cultivars grow very tall (e.g. 'Alportii', 'Long White' and 'Tricolorifolia'). These are particularly suitable for cutting. Others are broad and spreading (e.g. 'Golden Rivulet' and 'Joan Sparkes'), or quite prostrate (e.g. 'Golden Carpet', 'Heidezwerg' and 'Mrs Ronald Gray'). Dwarf forms with a more or less spherical habit are 'Baby Wicklow', 'Foxii Nana' and 'Humpty Dumpty'.

In view of the very wide distribution of *Calluna*, it is understandable that not all its forms are winter-hardy. 'Elegantissima Walter Ingwersen', for example, as has been mentioned earlier, is not. But most others are.

Ericas

Variation is also great in the Ericas. Even among the 15 species that belong to the European flora, a wide difference is to be found in flowers, flowering time and growth. We can distinguish between the summer-flowering species (e.g. *Erica cinerea*, *E. tetralix* and *E. vagans*), and *E. carnea* that is a mass of flowers in winter and early spring. Some southern European species, e.g. *E. australis* and *E. umbellata*, flower only in late spring and early summer. As to growth, there are small prostrate plants only a few centimetres high; on the other hand there are the so-called tree heaths (including *E. arborea*) that can grow to a height of several metres.

In certain species there are cultivars with yellow or bronze-yellow foliage (e.g. *E. carnea* 'Aurea', *E. ciliaris* 'Aurea', *E. cinerea* 'Golden Drop' and *E. vagans* 'Valerie Proudley').

A spectacular range of colours can be found in the flowers. This is particularly striking in *E. cinerea*, which ranges from white through lilac, pink, salmon pink, magenta red, blood red, violet and purple to purple-black.

The inflorescence on the various *Erica* species also varies considerably. Thus *E. tetralix* typically bears its flowers in small, dense, terminal umbels, whereas *E. vagans*, for instance, has elongated racemes.

Double-flowered cultivars of any *Erica* are extremely rare. The only known hardy one, probably the only double *Erica* in cultivation at all, is *E. mackaiana* 'Plena'.

The species indigenous in Europe and their hybrids also differ in hardiness. *E. carnea* (from the mountains of central Europe), *E. cinerea* and *E. tetralix* (the last two, of course, natives) are the most resistant to frost.

E. × *darleyensis, E. mackaiana, E.* × *praegeri, E. terminalis, E.*

vagans, E. × *watsonii* and *E.* × *williamsii* may not do in the coldest districts; *E. ciliaris* and *E. erigena* may be rather less universally reliable, but all these can usually stand the worst of British winters. *E. lusitanica, E. scoparia* and *E. umbellata* are hardier than people think. *E. australis, E. arborea* and *E.* × *veitchii* can be cut down by hard frosts, but will generally sprout again from the base: none of the Mediterranean species is really suitable for cold areas, and *E. multiflora* and *E. manipuliflora* are unlikely to overwinter easily outside.

None of the more than 600 species that grow in South Africa and in the mountains of tropical Africa can stand up to our winters, except in the extreme south-west or in favoured parts of the west coast. However, for a specialist with a heated greenhouse it is well worth growing some of these beautiful Ericas.

How to tell Calluna from Erica

The most important morphological characters distinguishing *Calluna* from *Erica* are the leaf arrangement and the flower structure.

Calluna has leaves arranged 2 by 2, opposite and decussate and often overlapping. The calyx is markedly longer than the corolla, and usually of the same or a slightly darker colour. Both are divided into 4 segments which are united at the base; the calyx is usually more deeply divided than the corolla.

Erica has narrow leaves, often needle-like, in whorls of 3 or 4, sometimes 5 or 6. The calyx, consisting of 4 sepals, is shorter or much shorter than the corolla, which is usually deeply coloured and urn- or bell-shaped; the calyx is usually green or pale, but may be coloured.

Owing to the difference in flower structure, the flower colour of *Erica*, is almost wholly determined by the corolla, whereas the colour of *Calluna* is mainly determined by the larger calyx.

Key to the hardy species and hybrids of Calluna and Erica

First, take typical material, not from odd, drought-ridden or depauperate plants. All the species except *E. scoparia*, and all the hybrids except *E.* × *watsonii* and *E.* × *williamsii*, have been known with white flowers – albinos. The key also omits the tender *E. manipuliflora* and *E. multiflora* (p. 109, which differ from *E. vagans* in small characters. Sizes and blooming times relate to British conditions. For hybrids of starred species, see section 2a of the key.

To name a flowering heather, go down each set of contrasting characters, see which of the pair applies, and go on from that until the answer is reached, which must then be checked with the remarks later in the book, to which a page reference is given.

The number of leaves in a whorl has hardly been used in this key, because this is variable. Recorded numbers for the species are:

3. *arborea, ciliaris, cinerea* (young leaves only), *lusitanica, manipuliflora, scoparia, tetralix, umbellata.*
4. *arborea, australis, carnea, ciliaris, erigena, lusitanica, mackaiana, manipuliflora, multiflora, scoparia, terminalis, tetralix, vagans.*
5. *erigena, multiflora, terminalis, tetralix, vagans.*
6. *terminalis* – where really they may better be described as scattered up the stem – *tetralix.*

Naming heathers from non-flowering shoots can be a very uncertain process.

1. Leaves stubby in opposite, usually overlapping pairs (Fig 14A); calyx longer than the divided corolla and of the same, or a darker colour. Plants usually under 1 metre. Bloom June-Sept (-Dec).   CALLUNA (p. 83)

1a. Leaves narrow, often needle-like, in whorls of 3–6; calyx shorter than the usually undivided corolla and often green. Plants up to 4 metres. ERICA (p. 96) 2

2. Young leaves green. 3

2a Young leaves usually not green (hybrids); flowers purplish-pink. Other characters in general intermediate between those of the parents *qqv.* 16

3. Mature leaves hairy and ciliate, usually glandular; calyx lobes ciliate; anthers not protruding from the corolla; shrublets to 60 cm. Bloom June-Sept (-Nov). 4

3a. Mature leaves and calyx hairless or at most minutely ciliate. 6

4. Flowers typically in short umbel-shaped normally one-sided racemes; corolla ovoid 5–8 mm; anthers with two long appendages at the base (Fig. 14D). 5

4a. Flowers in racemes; corolla broad tubular 8–11 mm; anthers without appendages (Fig. 14C); ovary hairless.
*E. ciliaris** (p. 101)

5. Leaves below the inflorescence sparse and usually erect; calyx and ovary pubescent (Fig. 14D).
*E. tetralix** (p. 111)

5a. Leaves below inflorescence dense and spreading; calyx ciliate only, ovary hairless. *E. mackaiana** (p. 108)

6. Flowers usually whitish in pyramidal clusters; anthers not protruding, with appendages; ovary hairless. Bloom in spring. 7

6a. Flowers coloured. 8

7. Corolla bell-shaped, ashy-white (rarely pale pink) 2–4 mm on longer stalks; stigma broad usually white; hairs branched (× 15 lens!). Bloom March-June. Shrub or small tree to 4 m or more. *E. arborea* (p. 96)

7a. Corolla cylindrical, pink in bud, maturing white 4–5 mm on stalks of the same length; stigma narrow, usually red; hairs unbranched. Bloom (Sept-) Feb-June. Shrub to 2.5 m *E. lusitanica* (p. 107)

7 *Erica cinerea* 'C. D. Eason'

Calluna vulgaris 'Silver Queen' – *Erica* × *veitchii* 'Exeter' (behind)

8 A heather garden in a thinned out pinewood

Erica tetralix 'Helma'

Erica carnea 'Myretoun Ruby'

A group of mixed *Erica carnea*

7b. Characters intermediate between the last two
$E. \times veitchii$ (p. 118)

8. Anthers not protruding (as in Fig. 14E).   9

8a. Anthers protruding (as in Fig 14B), without appendages, brown; ovary hairless.   13

9. Anthers with appendages (as in Fig. 14E).   10

9a. Anthers without appendages; tree heaths with insignificant greenish or brown spherical corollas to 5 mm; ovary hairless. Bloom Apr-June.   *E. scoparia* (p 110) 12

10. Tree heaths to 2.5 m; leaves usually in whorls of four; ovary pubescent.   11

10a. Dwarf shrub to 60 cm; young leaves in whorls of three, mature ones in bundles; flowers in racemes (Fig 14E); corolla 5–6 mm urn-shaped varying from pink to purple; ovary hairless. Bloom June-Sept.   *E. cinerera* (p. 102)

11. Flowers in umbels; corolla urn-shaped 5–6 mm, dusty pink; bloom June-Oct.   *E. terminalis* (p. 110)

11a. Flowers in clusters; corolla larger, showier, tubular, 6–9 mm, usually bright purple. Bloom May-June.
E. australis (p. 96)

12. Style not protruding; calyx $\frac{1}{2}$ length of corolla; habit open.   ssp. *scoparia* (p. 110)

12a. Style protruding; calyx $\frac{1}{3}$ length of corolla; habit denser, plant darker green.   ssp. *azorica* (p. 110)

13. Flowers in dense racemes, corolla bell-shaped, to 4 mm; anthers clearly divergent (Fig 14F); calyx lobes short, ovate, $\frac{1}{4}$–$\frac{1}{3}$ length of corolla; shrub to 80 cm. Bloom late summer.   *E. vagans** (p. 113)

13a. Flowers in less dense $\pm$ cylindrical inflorescences; corolla larger, anthers not divergent (Fig 14B); calyx lobes narrow $\frac{1}{3}$–$\frac{1}{2}$ length of corolla. Bloom in winter to early summer.   14

14. Flowers on hairless stalks not longer than the calyx, in racemes; corolla urn-shaped 5–6 mm. Bloom winter and spring.

14a. Flowers on pubescent stalks twice as long as the calyx, in umbels; corolla globose, to 5 mm. Spreading bush to 60 cm. Bloom Apr-June. *E. umbellata* (p. 113)

15. Prostrate, or small shrublet; flowers sometimes in very long racemes, to 17 cm. (Fig. 14B). Bloom (Oct-) Dec-April. *E. carnea** (p. 97)

15a. Taller shrub, to 1–2.5 m; flowers in racemes only up to 5 cm, anthers protruding less. Bloom Feb-May.
*E. erigena** (p. 107)

16. Leaves and calyx pubescent, anthers with short appendages. Bloom July-Sept. *E.* × *watsonii* (p. 119) 17

16a. Leaves much less, or not, hairy. 18

17. Hairs not gland-tipped. 'H. Maxwell' (p. 119)

17a. Hairs gland-tipped. all other cvs.

18. Anthers protruding; ovary hairless. Shrubs to 1 m. 19

18a. Anthers not or hardly protruding, without appendages; sepals and ovary slightly pubescent. Shrublet to 50 cm. Bloom July-Oct. 20

19. Young shoots pink or pale yellow; anthers without appendages. Bloom Jan-May. *E.* × *darleyensis* (p. 116) (racemes of 'Arthur Johnson' can exceed 20 cm, longer than in either parent)

19a. Young shoots yellow; anthers with short appendages; corolla, curiously, shorter than in either parent, 3–5 mm. Bloom July-Oct. *E.* × *williamsii* (p. 119)

20. Anthers not protruding; corolla ovoid pinkish concolorous, to 7 × 5 mm. *E.* × *praegeri* (p. 117)

20a. Anthers showing at mouth of tubular dark mauve-pink corolla, whitish at the base, to 6 × 2 mm.
E. 'Stuartii' (p. 118)

Calluna

* = a very valuable plant

CALLUNA VULGARIS (L.) Hull (1808)

Synonym: *Erica vulgaris* L. (1753)
English names: Ling, Heather, Scotch Heather.
Distribution: A great part of Europe, western Asia and North
Africa (see map on p. 85), naturalised in North America.
Description: A shrub 30–90(–200) cm high, sometimes with
prostrate or drooping branches. Leaves 1–3 mm, opposite,
decussate, glabrous or hairy. Flowers in racemes or paniculate
inflorescences, purple to pink; corolla small, shorter than the
calyx, and of the same or a paler colour; both divided into 4
segments united at the base. Blooming (June-) August-
September (-December).

'ALBA' – July-Aug., 50 cm
Flowers white; foliage rather light green; growth erect. Surpassed by better white cultivars. Is sometimes grown under the
name of 'Alba Erecta' or 'Elegantissima'.

'ALBA DUMOSA' (by 1877) – July-Aug., 40 cm
Flowers white; growth broad and spreading. Very similar to
'Alba Elegans' but flowers three to four weeks earlier. A good
plant, but 'Alba Praecox' is better.

'ALBA ERECTA' (by 1917) – Aug-Sept., 50 cm*
Flowers pure white; foliage vivid green; growth stiffly erect. A
beautiful plant, sometimes grown as the late-flowering 'Serlei'
(or 'Shirley'). It is also sold as 'Alba'.

83

'ALBA PLENA' (Bruns, 1934) – Aug-Oct., 40 cm*
Flowers pure white, double; growth broad and spreading,
graceful; a good ground-cover plant.
When propagating this double-flowered cultivar make sure
that the cutting material has double flowers. 'Alba Plena' may
revert to the single-flowered 'Alba Elegans', from which it
arose as a mutation.
'White Bouquet' is identical. 'Else Frye', an American seedling of quite distinct origin, differs little if at all.

'ALBA PRAECOX' (G. Arends, 1938) – June-Aug., 40 cm
Flowers pure white; foliage rather dark green; growth broad
erect. The newer 'Caerketton White' flowers about ten days
earlier.

'ALBA RIGIDA' (by 1867) – syn. 'Rigida Prostrata' –
July-Sept., 15 cm
Flowers white; foliage dark green; growth low and spreading
with short, stiff shoots.
Suitable for the rock garden and for small heather gardens.
Also known as 'Decumbens Alba'.

'ALPORTII' (England, 1838) – Aug-Sept., 70 cm
Flowers reddish purple; growth tall erect.
The early-flowering 'Alportii Praecox', grows to 40 cm. The
dwarfer 'Tenuis' is better.

'AUREA' (before 1835) – July-Sept., 40 cm
Flowers light purple-pink; foliage golden, in winter somewhat
brown-red. Older plants less handsomely coloured.
This old form has been superseded by more recent cultivars
such as 'Fairy' and 'Sunset'.
'Spitfire', introduced by Mr R. E. Hardwick, is very similar to
'Aurea', but they are not identical.

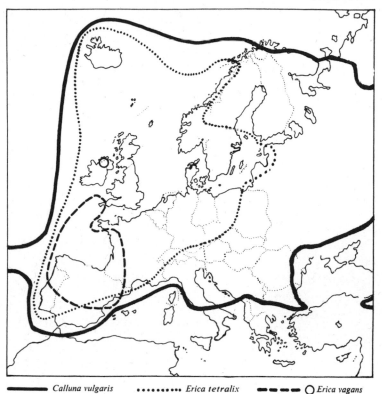

—— Calluna vulgaris •••••••• Erica tetralix ▬ ▬ ▬ ◯ Erica vagans

'BARNETT ANLEY' (England, before 1960) – Aug-Sept., 50 cm*
Flowers pure purple, long spikes; growth broad and tufted, a good ground coverer. A beautiful plant.
See plate 1.

'BEOLEY GOLD' (J. W. Sparkes, 1963) – Aug-Sept., 40 cm*
Flowers clear white, plentiful; foliage intense yellow, even in winter; growth erect.
An improvement on the better known 'Gold Haze'.

85

'BLAZEAWAY' (J. W. Sparkes, by 1963) – Aug-Sept., 45 cm*
Flowers a soft lilac-purple; foliage bronze-yellow, in winter
turning to bronzy red; growth broad erect.
Slightly less handsome but much more vigorous than 'Robert
Chapman'.

'BOSKOOP' (P. G. Zwijnenburg, 1972) – Aug-Sept., 40 cm*
Flowers light mauve-purple, exceptionally abundant; foliage
golden, in autumn and winter a bronzy orange-red; growth
broad erect.
Found as a seedling in the author's garden in 1967 and distributed in 1972.
See plate 1.

'CAERKETTON WHITE' (J. R. Ponton, 1957) – June-July,
30 cm
Flowers pure white, plentiful; only a short flowering season;
growth broad and low.
The earliest flowering *Calluna*.

'CARL RÖDERS' (H. Westermann, 1960) – Aug-Oct., 40 cm*
Flowers pure mauve-pink, plentiful; growth erect.
This was found on the Lüneburg Heath in Germany.

'CARMEN' (C. Bouter, 1968) – Aug-Sept., 40 cm*
Flowers purple-red, in long spikes, plentiful; foliage green;
growth broad erect.
Arose as a sport on 'Barnett Anley'. Can be considered a
lower-growing and broader 'C. W. Nix'. Very valuable.

'CHRISTINA' (A. H. Rijnbeek, 1970) – Sept-Oct., 50 cm
Flowers pure white; foliage green-yellow to yellow, in winter
bright yellow; growth erect, rather dense.
A distinctly yellower 'Serlei Aurea'. A fine foliage plant.

'COUNTY WICKLOW' (Maxwell & Beale, 1933) – Aug-Sept.,
25 cm

Flowers silvery pale pink, double; growth low, squat, unfortunately rather weak. A lovely cultivar but in bright sunny weather the flowers can quickly turn brown.

'CRAMOND' (S. Hall, 1963) – Sept-Nov., 50 cm*
Flowers deep pink, double; growth vigorous, broad erect.
A very good form; possibly an improvement on 'Peter Sparkes'.

'CUPREA' (before 1873) – Aug-Sept., 45 cm
Flowers light purple; foliage bronze-yellow, bronzy red-brown in winter; growth erect.
An old cultivar; now surpassed by many other foliage plants.

'C. W. NIX' (Maxwell & Beale, 1934) – Aug-Sept., 80 cm*
Flowers purple-red; growth tall erect, branches somewhat lax. Resembles 'Alportii'; can be distinguished by the rather redder flowers and the less erect tips to the branches.
See plate 10.

'DAINTY BESS' (U.S.A., 1962) – Aug-Sept., 10 cm
Flowers light purple-pink; foliage covered in bluish-grey hairs, downy; growth very low, prostrate. A curiosity.
Very similar to the English 'Sister Anne'; this grows slightly more vigorously and is less grey and hairy. Both may suffer from long periods of damp weather in autumn.

'DARKNESS' (Ness Gardens, by 1966) – Aug-Sept., 35 cm*
Flowers bright purple-red, in many-flowered racemes; growth erect, dense. A very beautiful new cultivar.
The alternative spelling, 'Dark Ness', is incorrect.
See plate 1.

'DARLEYENSIS' – syn. 'Brachysepala densa' (J. Smith & Sons by 1926) – Aug-Sept., 40 cm
Flowers mauve; foliage greyish green, bronze-coloured in winter, growth broad erect shoots somewhat curled much branched. A curious form.
Is similar to the less common 'Penhale'.

THE HEATHER GARDEN

'DAVID EASON' (Maxwell & Beale, 1948) – Sept-Nov.,
40 cm
Flower buds pure purple, hardly opening, later turning whitish; growth broad and spreading.

'DIRRY' (Driebergen Gardens, 1972) – Aug-Oct., 15 cm
Flowers reddish purple, in profusion; foliage dark green; growth spreading to prostrate, rather dense. Handsome. Found as a mutation on 'Mrs Ronald Gray' by H. J. Weber, Chief of the Heather Garden at Driebergen-Rijsenburg, Holland.

'DURFORDII' (1954) – Nov-Dec., 60 cm
Flowers light purple-pink, very late; usually a shy bloomer; foliage bronze-green, in winter blackish purple-brown; growth erect. An unusual plant.
Slightly earlier, and freer flowering, is the new Dutch 'Battle of Arnhem'. Even later is the wide-spreading 'Autumn Glow' that comes from America.

'ELEGANTISSIMA' (by 1906) – Aug-Sept., 50 cm
Flowers bright white; foliage grey-green, particularly in autumn; growth broad erect.
A plant with greener leaves, that in other respects is virtually the same, is 'Elegant Pearl'.
Not to be confused with the tender 'Elegantissima Walter Ingwersen', with light purple-pink flowers in October-December.

'ELSIE PURNELL' (J. W. Sparkes, before 1954) – Sept-Oct., 60 cm*
Flowers silvery pale pink, large, very double; growth broad erect.
An exceptionally graceful plant.
The flower colour is slightly lighter, the flower spikes stouter and the flowering time 1–2 weeks later than in the well-known 'H. E. Beale'.

88

'FAIRY' (J. W. Sparkes, 1966) – Aug-Sept., 40 cm*
Flowers a beautiful purple-pink; foliage golden, in winter a glowing red; growth erect, rather dense.
One of the most handsome foliage plants, particularly on sandy soil.

'FINALE' (J. F. Letts, by 1969) – Oct-Nov., 50 cm
Flowers pure purple; foliage fresh green, the young tips of the shoots grey-green; growth tall erect.
A late-flowering cultivar.

'FLORE PLENO' – syn. 'Plena' (England, before 1795) – Aug-Sept., 60 cm
Flowers a soft lilac-pink, double; growth broad erect.
A weak plant.
The first double cultivar recorded; flowers 2–3 weeks earlier than the better known 'H. E. Beale' and 'Peter Sparkes'.

'FOXII NANA' (1937) – July-Sept., 15 cm*
Flowers purple, often few; foliage dark green, bronze in winter; growth rounded and very compact.
One of the best dwarf forms; suitable for rock gardens.

'GOLDEN CARPET' (J. F. Letts, by 1966) – Aug-Sept.,8 cm*
Flowers light purple-pink, not very numerous; foliage a magnificent gold, in winter bronzey-brown (flecked); growth prostrate, very low.
A seedling in a group of 'Mrs Ronald Gray'. The new 'John F. Letts' grows slightly taller, but is otherwise similar. Both are good rock garden plants.

'GOLDEN RIVULET' (P. G. Davis, by 1970) – Aug-Sept., 25 cm*
Flowers very light purple; foliage golden, in winter bronze-red; growth low and broad.
An improvement on 'Golden Feather'. See plate 5.
An outstanding rock garden plant.
See plate 1.

'GOLD HAZE' (J. W. Sparkes, before 1961) – Aug-Sept., 50 cm*
Flowers white; foliage yellow, in winter a purer yellow; growth erect.
The colour of the foliage is slightly less yellow than that of the newer 'Beoley Gold'. 'Gold Haze' flowers less prolifically when it is a young plant; some people consider this to be an advantage.
See plate 5.

'HAMMONDII' – syn. 'Alba Hammondii' (Britain, by 1850) – Aug-Sept., 60 cm
Flowers white; foliage a fine dark green, contrasting well with the pure white flowers; growth vigorously erect.
'Hammondii Aureifolia' has pale yellow young growth in spring; 'Hammondii Rubrifolia', in contrast, has reddish tips and blooms very prolifically with light purple flowers.

'H. E. BEALE' (Maxwell & Beale, c.1926) – Sept-Oct., 60 cm*
Flowers silvery lilac-pink, double, in much branched racemes; growth broad and erect.
A very fine, widely grown cultivar. Has been partially superseded by the newer 'Cramond', 'Elsie Purnell' and 'Peter Sparkes'. All are outstanding for use as dried flowers.
See plate 1.

'HEIDEZWERG' (F. Kircher, 1953) – Aug-Sept., 8 cm
Flowers purple, rather sparse; foliage delicate, light green with a somewhat purple-brown tint; growth prostrate, mat-forming.
A fine German cultivar, highly recommended.

'HUMPTY DUMPTY' (J. W. Sparkes, pre 1963) – Aug-Sept., 20 cm
Flowers white, very few, none on young plants; foliage light

green (moss green); growth very dense, broad and low.
An interesting, slow-growing dwarf. A curiosity.

'INEKE' (W. Veldink, 1971) – Aug-Sept., 40 cm
Flowers light purple; foliage a striking pale yellow, later green-yellow, in winter bronzy green; growth broad erect, lax.
An attractive new cultivar; quite different from all other yellow-leaved plants. Found on the Stroese Zand (Veluwe), Holland.

'J. H. HAMILTON' (Maxwell & Beale, before 1932) – Aug-Sept., 25 cm*
Flowers pure salmon pink, double; foliage dark bronze-green in winter; growth low and spreading.
The only *Calluna* with salmon pink flowers. Highly recommended; also suitable for use dried.

'LONG WHITE' (W. Haalboom & Sons, 1962) – Sept-Oct., 70 cm*
Flowers pure white, in long racemes; foliage fresh green; growth vigorously erect.
This healthy and strong growing *Calluna* must be pruned regularly or it soon gets straggly. Very good for cutting. A good substitute for the slightly later-flowering 'Serlei'. Found in a batch of cuttings in the nursery of the municipal Heather Garden in Driebergen-Rijsenburg, and distributed by W. Haalboom & Sons.

'MINIMA SMITH'S VARIETY' (T. Smith of Newry, before 1940) – July-Sept., 15 cm
Flowers light purple-pink, in plenty; foliage light green, in winter rusty brown; growth mat-forming, rather compact.
Flowers much more prolifically than the old, better known 'Minima'.
A very beautiful form.

'MRS RONALD GRAY' (Maxwell & Beale, 1933) – Aug-Oct., 8 cm*

Flowers pure purple, in horizontal racemes; foliage bright green; growth very low, prostrate.

One of the best low Callunas; very suitable for rockeries and between large flagstones.

See plate 5.

'MULLION' (Maxwell & Beale, 1923) – Aug-Sept., 25 cm*
Flowers deep mauve-purple, on much branched shoots; growth compact, somewhat prostrate or mat-forming.

A highly recommended, freely flowering dwarf.

The similar cultivar, 'Kynance', has mauve-pink flowers.

See plate 1.

'MULTICOLOR' – syn. 'Prairie Fire' (U.S.A., by 1938) – July-Sept., 20 cm*
Flowers light purple; foliage bronzy green-yellow, in winter a magnificent red; growth broad and spreading to more or less erect.

A splendid healthy plant which, unfortunately, often reverts to green shoots, which need to be cut out regularly.

'NANA COMPACTA' (by 1930) – Aug-Sept., 20 cm*
Flowers purple-pink, in plenty; foliage soft green; growth rounded, rather dense.

Recommended for small gardens. Is sometimes grown under the name of 'Foxii Floribunda'.

'ORANGE QUEEN' (J. W. Sparkes, 1965) – Aug-Sept., 50 cm*
Flowers mauve-pink; foliage yellow to golden, in winter orange; growth broad erect.

'PETER SPARKES' (J. W. Sparkes, 1955) – Sept-Oct., 60 cm*
Flowers a silvery deep pink, double; growth broad erect.

A sport of 'H. E. Beale' that flowers at about the same time, with purer pink, slightly darker flowers. Very beautiful, especially suitable for drying.

'PROSTRATA FLAGELLIFORMIS' (H. A. Hesse, by 1935) –
Aug-Sept., 8 cm
Flowers purple-pink; foliage dull green; growth very low,
prostrate with down-curved shoot tips.
Very similar to 'Kuphaldtii', but grows less tall and broad and
is more delicate. 'Heidezwerg' resembles both.

'RADNOR' – syn. 'Miss Appleby' (Appleby, c.1954) –
Aug-Sept., 25 cm*
Flowers light pink, double; low and broad with erect shoots.
Can be considered an improved 'County Wicklow'.

'RALPH PURNELL' (J. W. Sparkes, c.1960) – Aug-Sept.,
60 cm*
Flowers pure purple, sometimes rather tinged with pink, in
many-flowered, erect racemes; growth vigorously erect.
A beautiful plant for cutting; flowers prolifically but for no
longer than about three weeks.
See plate 5.

'ROBERT CHAPMAN' (J. W. Sparkes, c.1960) – Aug-Sept.,
40 cm
Flowers purple-pink; foliage a magnificent bronze-yellow,
later light orange, in winter a glorious bronze-red; growth
broad erect.
An exceptionally fine foliage plant, in both summer and winter.
'Blazeaway' is not quite so beautiful, but much stronger.
Possibly 'Boskoop', 'Sir John Charrington' and 'Sunset' would
be good alternatives.

'RUTH SPARKES' (J. W. Sparkes, 1951) – Aug-Sept., 25 cm
Flowers white, double; foliage pure yellow, even in winter;
growth broad and spreading, low and rather dense.
This pure yellow sport of 'Alba Plena' may produce reversions
with green shoots. If these are regularly removed, it is still
worth planting this cultivar.

93

'Dart's Gold', a mutation with even yellower foliage, more compact growth and single flowers, was introduced in 1972 by Darthuizer Nurseries, Leersum, Holland.

'SERLEI' – syn. 'Alba Serlei'; 'Searlei' (by 1867) – Sept-Oct., 70 cm

Flowers pure white, in long racemes; foliage rather greyish green; growth vigorously erect.

The latest flowering white *Calluna*; unfortunately it is rather susceptible to disease. A good substitute is the slightly earlier flowering 'Long White'.

The plants that a few years ago were exported as 'Serlei' in large numbers from Dutch nurseries were nearly always 'Alba Erecta', a cultivar that flowers about one month earlier.

'SERLEI AUREA' (*c*.1937) – Sept-Oct., 50 cm

Flowers pure white; foliage yellowish green, in winter distinctly yellower; growth erect, rather dense.

A number of plants with more or less yellow foliage are grown under this name. There are also the greener-leaved 'Serlei Grandiflora Alba' and the new, much yellower 'Christina'. All are specifically foliage plants.

'SILVER QUEEN' (by 1937) – Aug-Sept., 40 cm*

Flowers mauve, plentiful; foliage strikingly covered with a thick coating of silver-grey hairs; growth broad and spreading with erect shoots.

An interesting foliage plant, particularly in combination with other plants that have beautiful leaf colours. Stands up reasonably well to drought.

In England it is usually grown as 'Hirsuta Typica'. The plants that are grown under this name, or as 'Hirsuta', in Holland, are much less thickly covered with grey hairs.

See plates 5 and 7.

'SIR JOHN CHARRINGTON' (J. W. Sparkes, 1966) –
Aug-Sept., 30 cm
Flowers deep purple-red, later turning purple; foliage golden,
in winter a glorious deep red; growth very broad.
A new cultivar.

'SUMMER ORANGE' (J. W. Sparkes, by 1966) – Aug-Sept.,
40 cm
Flowers purple-pink; foliage orange-yellow, in winter turning
to pure orange; growth broad erect.

'SUNSET' (J. W. Sparkes, by 1963) – Aug-Sept., 30 cm*
Flowers purple-pink; foliage bronze-yellow, in winter a bril-
liant bronze-red; growth broad and spreading.
One of the best yellow-leaved cultivars.

'TENUIS' (by 1827) – June-Nov., 25 cm
Flowers purple-red, large; growth broad and low, a fairly good
ground-cover plant. A dwarf form.
One of the earliest flowering Callunas; with a few breaks, it
blooms right through into November.

'TIB' (Maxwell & Beale, 1938) – June-Sept., 40 cm*
Flowers pure purple, double, small, very prolific; growth
erect. The earliest of the double-flowered cultivars.

'UNDERWOODII' (G. Underwood & Son, c.1936) –
Sept–Dec., 45 cm*
Flower buds silvery purple, never opening, later turning sil-
very white; shoots thin and graceful; growth erect.
A curious plant with buds that do not open, but give a colour
effect right into December.
In 1972 Dr T. Visser, of Wageningen, named several similar
plants that were found in Holland. These are 'Adrie', 'Ginkel's
Glorie', 'Marilyn' and 'Marleen'. They were introduced by
W. Haalboom & Sons, Driebergen, Holland.

Erica

* = a very valuable plant

ERICA ARBOREA L. (1753)

English name: Tree Heath.
Distribution: Mediterranean area and East Africa.
Description: A tall shrub or small tree of 2–4 (–6) m. Leaves in whorls of 3 (–4). Flowers bell-shaped, greyish white to sometimes very pale pink, in terminal panicles. Blooming April–May. In hard winters it can be cut back by frost but usually sprouts again.

'ALPINA' – Apr-May, 150 (–180) cm
Flowers white, in large clusters; foliage fresh green; growth more erect than the typical form and rather dense. Hardier. See plate 9.

'ESTRELLA GOLD' (P. G. Zwijnenburg, 1974) – Apr-May, 100–150 cm.
Flowers white; foliage pure bronze-yellow to greenish yellow; growth tall erect.
Found in the Serra da Estrela to the East of Coimbra, Portugal.

ERICA AUSTRALIS L. (1770)

English name: Southern Tree Heath.
Distribution: Spain, Portugal and Morocco; the var. *aragonensis* Willk. (1852) in north-west Spain and north Portugal.

96

Description: A shrub 1 (-2.5) m high. Leaves in whorls of 4. Flowers bright purple, tubular, in terminal clusters. Blooming May-June. Not fully hardy in cold districts.

'Mr Robert' is a cultivar with pure white flowers and dark green foliage.

ERICA CARNEA L. (1753)[1]

Synonyms: Erica herbacea L. (1753); *Erica mediterranea* L., non Hort.

English name: Winter Heath.

Distribution: Central and southern Europe (Alps, Apennines, Germany, Yugoslavia and the north-western Balkan Peninsula), (see map on p. 98).

Description: A shrublet up to 20 cm high, often partially procumbent. Leaves in whorls of 4. Flowers nodding, urn-shaped, purple-pink, in one-sided racemes. Blooming (October-) December-April. Very hardy. Several clones in cultivation are known as plain *Erica carnea*. (See plate 8.)

'AUREA' (by 1928) – Feb-Apr., 20 cm.
Flowers purple-pink; foliage golden, in winter bronzy green. An attractive foliage plant.

'FOXHOLLOW' (J. F. Letts, by 1969) – Feb-Mar., 20 cm*
Flowers soft pink, sparse; foliage yellow to yellow-green, in winter bronze-yellow, in spring with pretty bronze-red tips. An improvement on the old, well-known 'Aurea'.

'HEATHWOOD' (J. H. Brummage, 1963) – Mar-Apr., 25 cm*
Flowers dull, dark purple-pink; foliage sometimes bronzy green. Very similar to 'Loughrigg' but has a lower, more compact growth and can therefore be more highly recommended.

1 For good reasons the name *Erica carnea* should be retained, although *E. herbacea* is used in *Flora Europaea*.

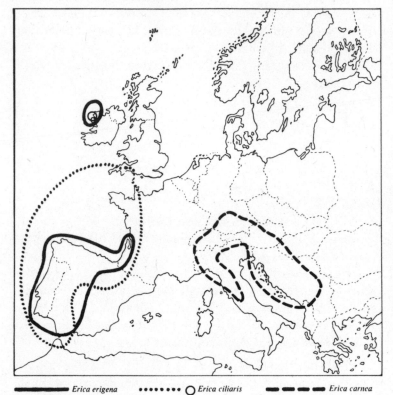

| ▬▬▬▬ Erica erigena | •••••• ○ Erica ciliaris | ▬ ▬ ▬ Erica carnea |

'JAMES BACKHOUSE' (J. Backhouse, 1911) – Mar-Apr., 25 cm
Flowers pale purple-pink, large; foliage bright green. One of the best old, pale-coloured cultivars.

'KING GEORGE' (J. Backhouse, 1911) – Dec-Mar., 15 cm*
Flowers dark purple-pink, plentiful; growth very compact.
A splendid, healthy plant, flowering freely and early. One of the most widely grown cultivars in Europe.
The plants grown in Holland and other countries under the name of 'Winter Beauty' are identical with English 'King

George' and, according to John F. Letts, should be called 'King George'. Letts' 'Winter Beauty' does, in fact, differ from 'King George', but it still remains to be seen whether it has any value. It appears to be weaker and laxer in growth and for this reason has tended to disappear from cultivation.

'MYRETOUN RUBY' – syn. 'Winter Jewel' (A. Porteous, *c*.1960) – Mar-Apr., 20 cm*
Flowers an intense wine-red, large; foliage dark green; growth broad and spreading.
An outstanding new cultivar; the flower colour is significantly redder than that of the very well known 'red' 'Vivellii'. Particularly recommended.
See plate 8.

'PINK SPANGLES' (Treseder's Nurseries, 1966) – Feb-Apr., 30 cm*
Flowers a bright deep pink, very large and borne in profusion; growth vigorous, broad and lax.
An exceptionally fine new cultivar. Highly recommended for larger areas. Was brought on the market by Treseders as *Erica* × *darleyensis* 'Pink Spangles'.
See plate 9.

'PRAECOX RUBRA' – syn. 'Rubra' (J. Backhouse, 1911) – Nov-Mar., 20 cm*
Flowers light purple-red; foliage dark green; broad, spreading habit.
A well-known, very beautiful, exceptionally early-flowering cultivar.
See plate 4.

'RUBY GLOW' – syn. 'Atrorubra' (before 1932) – Feb-Apr., 20 cm*
Flowers deep purple-pink, large; foliage dark green.
One of the finest cultivars, with strikingly coloured flowers. Highly recommended.

The plants found in some nurseries as 'Rosy Gem' (a corruption of 'Ruby Glow'?) are exactly the same as 'Ruby Glow'.

'SNOW QUEEN' (Verboom Bros, 1934) – Dec-Mar., 15 cm
Flowers pure white, large, plentiful; foliage fresh green; growth low and open with rather lax shoots.
The older English 'Cecilia M. Beale' is often confused with this. It has a more rounded habit and stiffer shoots. It flowers about one month later, but is much easier to grow.

'SPRINGWOOD PINK' (Walker, 1931) – Feb-Apr., 20 cm
Flowers light purple-pink, large; growth spreading with long stems, mat-forming.
A seedling of 'Springwood White'. 'Pink Spangles' is a great improvement on this.

'SPRINGWOOD WHITE' – syn. 'Springwood' (Walker, 1930 – Feb-Apr., 25 cm
Flowers pure white, large; growth spreading with rather untidy stems, mat-forming. A good ground-cover plant.
Found on the Monte Carreggio in Italy by Mrs Ralph Walker, Springwood, Stirling, Scotland.
See plate 4.

'VIVELLII' (P. Theoboldt, 1906) – (Feb.–) Mar-Apr., 20 cm*
Flowers purple-red; foliage dark bronze, particularly in winter. A very ornamental plant, but unfortunately rather weak and therefore often difficult to grow. Found in the Engadin by Paul Theoboldt, propagated in 1909 in his own nursery in Württemberg and named after the head of his former firm, A. Vivell, of Olten, Switzerland. 'Urville' is exactly the same as this. The name doubtless arose as a clerical error.

'WINTER BEAUTY' – See under 'King George'

ERICA CILIARIS L. (1753)

English name: Dorset Heath.

Distribution: South-western England (Cornwall, Devon, Dorset), western Ireland (Co. Galway), western France, north-western and southern Spain, Portugal and Morocco (see map on p. 98).

Description: A shrub up to 60 cm high, with often procumbent shoots. Leaves in whorls of 3 (–4), hairy (usually ciliate with glandular hairs). Flowers broad tubular, mauve-pink, in elongated racemes, 5–12 cm long. Blooming (July-) August-September (-November).

'CAMLA' (W. E. Th. Ingwersen, 1934) – July-Oct., 35 cm
Flowers purple-pink, large; foliage green, coarse; growth broad and tufted.
A beautiful cultivar.

'CORFE CASTLE' (G. Osmond, *c.*1962) – July-Sept., 30 cm*
Flowers salmony pinky red; foliage bronze-green in winter; growth very broad to erect.
An exceptionally fine new cultivar; the flower colour is very distinctive.

'DAVID MCCLINTOCK' (Proudleys' Heather Nursery, 1969) – July-Oct., 40 cm*
Flowers white, violet-pink near the tip of the corolla (bi-coloured), later turning pink all over; foliage greyish green; growth very wide with erect shoots.
Found in 1962 near Carnac (Brittany), France; named after the finder.
A beautiful new acquisition.

'GLOBOSA' (Maxwell & Beale, by 1925) – July-Oct., 35 cm*
Flowers mauve-pink, in great plenty; foliage greyish green; growth broad erect.
Shortly after, by 1929 and 1933, Maxwell & Beale also in-

troduced the cultivars 'Norden' and 'Rotundiflora'. Some material grown in Holland under these names is exactly the same as 'Globosa'.

'STOBOROUGH' (Maxwell & Beale, 1927) – Aug-Oct., 60 cm
Flowers pure white, large, in long racemes; foliage dark green; growth vigorously erect.
The best white cultivar, finer than 'Alba' and 'White Wings'; a sport of the pinky red 'Mrs C. H. Gill'.

ERICA CINEREA L. (1753)

English name: Bell Heather.
Distribution: South-western Norway, Great Britain, Ireland, Belgium, Holland (province of Limburg), Germany (north-western Rhine province), north-western Italy, France, northern Spain and Portugal.
See map on p. 108.
Description: A broad erect shrub up to 60 cm high. Young leaves in whorls of 3, later in bundles, glabrous to slightly hairy. Flowers typically purplish pink, urn-shaped, in oblong racemes, often branched and so broad and loose, sometimes compact (cylindrical). Blooming June-Sept (-Oct).

'ALBA' Aug-Sept., 25 cm*
Flowers pure white in long racemes; foliage green; growth very broad with rather pendulous branches.

'ALBA MINOR' (by 1851) – June-Oct., 18 cm*
Flowers white in short racemes; foliage light green; growth short and tufted.
A very early-flowering form, starting in June and, with a few breaks, continuing into October. An old cultivar.
See plate 4.

'ATRORUBENS' (1915) – July-Oct., 25 cm
Flowers a glowing pinky red, plentiful; growth broad erect. Is sometimes sold for 'Rosea' (q.v.).
See plate 4.

'ATROSANGUINEA REUTHE'S VARIETY' (G. Reuthe, c.1926) – June-Aug., 12 cm
Flowers deep carmine red (blood red); foliage dark green; growth very low, more or less prostrate. Rare.

'ATROSANGUINEA SMITH'S VARIETY (J. Smith & Sons, c.1852) – July-Oct., 20 cm*
Flowers a glowing pinky red, very striking; foliage bright green; growth wide and spreading with erect shoots.
An exceptionally fine, free-flowering form. Quite widely grown.

'C. D. EASON' (Maxwell & Beale, 1931) – June-Sept., 35 cm*
Flowers vivid magenta red (pinky-red); foliage dark green; growth broad erect.
One of the most widely grown cultivars, very beautiful. Has been seen in Holland under 15 different names, for example 'Atropurpurea', 'Atrorubens', 'C. E. Pearson', 'Coccinea', 'Fulgida', 'Rosabella', 'Rosea' and 'Splendens'.
See plates 4 and 7.

'CEVENNES' (Wisley Gardens, c.1935) – Aug-Oct., 25 cm
Flowers lavender pink, in stiff erect racemes; growth erect.
A very beautiful, free-flowering form; may prove tender in some parts.
Found about 1930 by Sir O. Warburg in the Cevennes in France.

'C. G. BEST' (Maxwell & Beale, 1931) – Aug-Sept., 40 cm
Flowers salmon pink, in very long racemes, foliage rather grey-green; growth erect, open.
The best cultivar in this colour; recommended.

'COCCINEA' (J. Smith & Sons, c.1852) – June-Aug., 18 cm*
Flowers deep carmine red (blood red); foliage dark green;
growth broad erect with somewhat prostrate shoots. A rather
rare, very decorative plant.
Very similar to 'Atrosanguinea Reuthe's Variety'. According
to Letts 'Coccinea' is dwarfer; in Holland the opposite is true.
See plate 9.

'FOXHOLLOW MAHOGANY' (J. F. Letts, c.1964) –
July-Sept., 30 cm
Flowers a dull wine-red, plentiful; foliage dark green; growth
spreading to erect, loose, somewhat lax.
A very distinctive colour for *Erica cinerea*. Can be considered
better than 'Joyce Burfitt'. This latter is unfortunately weak;
its flowers are a salmony brown-pink.

'GOLDEN DROP' (Maxwell & Beale, 1933) – July-Aug.,
15 cm
Flowers purple-pink, produced very sporadically; foliage
bronzy golden, in winter a reddish rusty brown; growth very
compact, broad to prostrate.
An exceptionally fine form; it sometimes makes weak growth.
See plate 9.

'G. OSMOND' (Maxwell & Beale, 1931) – July-Sept., 35 cm*
Flowers a very pale mauve, racemes long; growth erect.
A distinctive cultivar; the very pale flower colour is beautiful
in combination with darker ones like 'Katinka' and 'Velvet
Night'.

'GRANDIFLORA' (by 1867) – July-Aug., 35 cm*
Flowers pure purple, very large in long racemes; growth broad
with more or less erect shoots.
An old, free-flowering cultivar.

'KATINKA' (Driebergen Gardens, 1968) – June-Sept., 30 cm
Flowers blackish purple; foliage dark green; growth erect.
Has the darkest colour in this group. Very similar to the Eng-

lish 'Velvet Night', which blooms less freely when the plants are young and grows slightly taller; moreover, the colour of the flowers is slightly 'redder'.

'PALLAS' (Dutch Growers, 1970) – June-Sept., 35 cm*
Flowers pure purple, borne in profusion; growth broad erect.
In Holland this has been cultivated for a long time under the incorrect name of 'Pallida'. In 1970 it was given the new name of 'Pallas'. The true 'Pallida' has very light (pale) lavender-pink flowers.

'PALLIDA' (Maxwell & Beale, 1927) – July-Sept., 30 cm
Flowers very light (pale) lavender-pink; growth erect.
A fine form; like 'G. Osmond', it makes an attractive combination with dark-coloured cultivars. See note under 'Pallas'.

'PINK ICE' (J. F. Letts, before 1966) – June-Sept., 20 cm*
Flowers pure pink, large, plentiful; foliage bronze-green at first, later dark green; growth compact, broader than it is tall.
A fine new garden form; the pink flowers contrast very well with the dark foliage.

'PLUMMER'S SEEDLING' (J. E. B. Plummer, 1960) –
June-Aug., 25 cm
Flowers very deep red, plentiful; growth broad erect, loose.
A plant that is still not very well known, but can be recommended.

'P. S. PATRICK' (Maxwell & Beale, c.1928) – Aug-Sept., 40 cm*
Flowers a lively violet-purple in long racemes; growth vigorously erect, slender.
One of the best purple cultivars.

'PYGMAEA' (G. Reuthe, before 1908) – June-Aug., 15 cm
Flowers bright magenta red (pinky red); growth more or less prostrate, low.
One of the earliest flowering cultivars; the colour is very much the same as that of 'C. D. Eason'.

In 1925 'Mrs Dill' was introduced by T. Smith of Newry, Northern Ireland. According to Letts this grows only 10 cm high. The plant that is grown in Holland under this name is identical with 'Pygmaea'.

'ROSEA' (Waterer, c.1867) – June-Sept., 25 cm*
Flowers bright carmine pink; growth dense and tufted.
A very old cultivar. Often found in Dutch nurseries under the names of 'Atrorubens' or 'Rosabella'.
'Knap Hill' can be considered an improved 'Rosea'.

f. *schizopetala* (Maxwell & Beale, 1934) – July-Oct., 35 cm
Flowers light mauve; the corolla is divided into 4 segments; growth erect, loose. An attractive form.
'W. G. Notley' and 'Winifred Whitley' also have divided corollas.

'SMITH'S LAWN' (before 1963) – July-Aug., 30 cm
Flowers a very light lavender colour with a slight purple tinge, in long racemes; foliage fresh green; growth broad erect, compact.
A very free-flowering plant with a distinctive colour rather like that of 'Pallida'.

'STEPHEN DAVIS' (P. G. Davis, 1969) – June-Aug., 25 cm*
Flowers an intense pinky red (deep magenta red), plentiful; foliage dark green; growth broad erect, fairly compact.
One of the best new introductions, an improved 'C. D. Eason'. Highly recommended.

Erica codonodes – See *E. lusitanica*

Erica corsica – See *E. terminalis*

ERICA ERIGENA R. Ross (1969)

Synonyms: E. mediterranea Hort., non L.; *E. hibernica* (Hook. and Arn.) Syme, non Utinct; *E. carnea* L. ssp. *occidentalis* (Benth.) Lainz.
English name: Irish Heath.
Distribution: Western Ireland, south-western France (Gironde), Spain and Portugal (see map on p. 98).
Description: A shrub 1–2.5 m high. Leaves in whorls of 4 (–5), glabrous.
Flowers in short racemes, urn-shaped, nodding, light purple-pink. Blooming February-May. Quite hardy.
Good cultivars are: 'Brightness' (bright purple-pink; 125 cm), 'Irish Salmon' (pink; 125 cm), 'Superba' (dark purple-pink; 250 cm) and 'W. T. Rackliff' (pure white; 150 cm).

Erica herbacea – See *E. carnea*

Erica hibernica – See *E. erigena*

ERICA LUSITANICA Rud. (1799)

Synonym: E. codonodes Lindl.
English name: Spanish Heath.
Distribution: Portugal, north-western Spain and south-western France (Gironde); naturalised in north-western France, south-western England and in New Zealand.
Description: An erect shrub of 1 (–3) m. Leaves in whorls of 3 (–4). Flowers in pyramidal clusters, cylindrical, pink in bud, later white. Blooming (September-) February-June. Quite hardy.

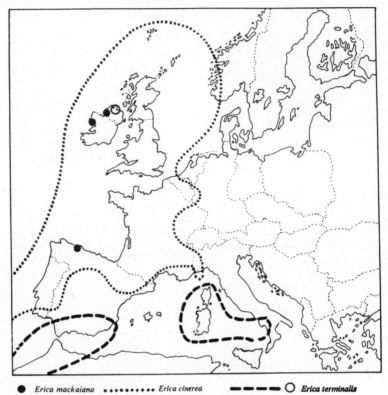

● *Erica mackaiana* ••••••••• *Erica cinerea* ▬ ▬ ▬ O *Erica terminalis*

ERICA MACKAIANA Bab. (1836)

Synonyms: E. mackaii Hook.; *E. tetralix* L. 'Mackaiana'.
English name: Mackay's Heath.
Distribution: Western Ireland and north-western Spain (see map above).
Description: A procumbent to erect small shrub, 10–30 cm, in Spain sometimes as high as 80 cm (among other shrubs). Leaves in whorls of 4, dark green, ciliate. Flowers ovoid, mauve-pink in small, dense, terminal umbels. Blooming July-September. Generally hardy.

'LAWSONIANA' (Lawson & Sons, c.1880) – July-Sept., 15 cm
Flowers light mauve-pink; foliage soft green; growth very
broad.

'PLENA' (Crawford, 1901) – July-Sept., 15 cm
Flowers bright lilac-pink, fully double, the only double hardy
Erica; growth spreading, procumbent.
A very beautiful cultivar.

'WM M'ALLA' (1834) – July–Sept., 15 cm
Flowers deep mauve-pink; foliage dark green; growth very
broad.
This is what has been grown for many years as plain *Erica
mackaiana*.

ERICA MANIPULIFLORA Salisb. (1802)

Synonym: E. verticillata Forsk., non Berg.
English name: Whorled Heath.
Distribution: Eastern Mediterranean area (Istria, Dalmatia,
southern Italy, Albania and Greece) and Asia Minor (coastal
region) to Syria, Lebanon and Israel.
Description: A small shrub of 50–80 cm. Leaves in whorls of 3 or
4. Flowers bell-shaped, pink, in open terminal, rather sparse
racemes. Blooming August-October. Not hardy.

Erica mediterranea Hort. – See *E. erigena*

Erica mediterranea L. – See *E. carnea*

Erica mediterranea hybrida – See *E.* × *darleyensis*

ERICA MULTIFLORA L. (1753)

English name. Many-flowered Heath
Distribution: Southern Europe (central Mediterranean area)
and North Africa.

Description: A small shrub of 80 cm or so. Leaves in whorls of 4 or 5. Flowers bell-shaped, pink, in short racemes, rarely up to 10 cm long, anthers parallel. Blooming November-February. Not really hardy.

ERICA SCOPARIA L. (1753)

English name: Besom Heath.
Distribution: France, Spain, Portugal, Corsica, Sardinia, western Italy, North Africa (from Morocco to Tunis), Canary Islands and Madeira.

Description: An irregular, loose, erect shrub 0.5–1 (–3) m high. Leaves in whorls of 3 (–4). Flowers spherical, very small, greenish, in a thin, short-branched raceme. Blooming April-June. Moderately hardy.
ssp. *azorica* (Hochst. ex Seub.) Webb (syn. *E. azorica* Hochst. ex Seub. 1844) is the subspecies (or, if you like, species) from the Azores (for ssp. *scoparia* see p. 63).

Erica stricta – See *E. terminalis*

ERICA TERMINALIS Salisb. (1796)

Synonyms: *E. stricta* Donn ex Willd.; *E. corsica* DC.
English name: Corsican Heath.
Distribution: Corsica, Sardinia, southern Spain, Italy, North Africa (north-western Morocco) (see map on p. 108); a well established garden escape in Northern Ireland.
Description: An erect, rather stiff shrub of 1 (–2.5) m. Leaves in whorls of 4 (sometimes 5 or 6). Flowers urn-shaped, dusty pink, in terminal umbels. Blooming June-October.

ERICA TETRALIX L. (1753)

English name: Cross-leaved Heath.

Distribution: Central Norway, southern Sweden, Great Britain, Ireland, Denmark, the Baltic region, north-western Germany, Holland, Belgium, northern and western France to central Portugal and Spain (see map on p. 85); naturalised in North America

Description: An erect, later often procumbent, small shrub of 40 (–70) cm. Leaves in whorls of 4 (–6), usually with glandular hairs. Flowers ovoid, light pink to mauve-pink, typically in terminal, one-sided umbels, or a number together forming a larger umbel. Blooming June-October.

'ALBA' – June-Sept., 30 cm*
Flowers pure white, in bud creamy white, rather small; foliage covered with silver-grey hairs (not glandular!), even in winter. A beautiful foliage plant.
Widely grown, in England always as 'Alba Mollis' which, in all probability, is incorrect.

'ALBA MOLLIS' – June-Sept., 30 cm
Flowers white, often turning to very pale pink as the flowers go over, large; foliage grey-green, covered with downy hairs (glandular!). An old cultivar, widely known in Holland, but very rare in England.
The plants in England under this name are identical with what is grown in Holland as 'Alba'.
'Alba Praecox' flowers as early as the beginning of June. The foliage is greyish light green in colour and covered in soft glandular hairs.

'ARDY' (P. G. Zwijnenburg, 1974) – June-Aug., 25 cm
Flowers deep pinky red, small; foliage dark grey-green; growth broad erect.
A mutation on 'Daphne Underwood' with slightly smaller

flowers of a striking red; the reddest in the *E. tetralix* range.
Found in 1968 in the author's garden.
See plate 12.

'CON UNDERWOOD' (G. Underwood & Son, 1938) –
July-Sept., 35 cm*
Flowers dull carmine red, plentiful; foliage grey-green.
A cultivar that grows well and can be highly recommended.

'DAPHNE UNDERWOOD' (G. Underwood & Son, 1953) –
June-Aug., 25 cm
Flowers bright pinky red, plentiful; foliage dark grey-green.
A beautiful plant, but the growth is rather weak.

'HELMA' (P. G. Zwijnenburg, 1967) – July-Sept., 40 cm*
Flowers mauve-pink, pointing horizontally all round; growth
erect, tall.
A beautiful, very free-flowering form; unusual in its horizontal
flowers.
Found in 1965 on a heath in the nature reserve 'Kampina'
between Boxtel and Tilburg in Holland.
See plate 8.

'HOOKSTONE PINK' (G. Underwood & Son, 1953) –
June-Sept., 40 cm*
Flowers pure light pink; foliage silver-grey, even in winter;
growth vigorously erect.
An exceptionally good form because it flowers freely, early and
over a long period.

'KEN UNDERWOOD' (G. Underwood & Son, 1951) –
June-Sept., 30 cm*
Flowers carmine pinky red, in plenty; foliage grey-green;
growth wide erect.
A plant that can be highly recommended, with an outstanding
flower colour.

9 *Erica cinerea* 'Coccinea'

Erica ciliaris 'Mrs. C. H. Gill'

Erica arborea 'Alpina'

Erica carnea 'Pink Spangles'

Erica tetralix 'Pink Star'

Erica cinerea 'Golden Drop'

10 A heather garden with a flagstone terrace

A garden with a group of *Calluna vulgaris* 'C. W. Nix'

'L. E. UNDERWOOD' (G. Underwood & Son, *c.*1937) – July-Sept., 30 cm

Flower buds brown-red; flowers light apricot pink; foliage bright (grey-) green; growth stiffly erect.

An attractive plant, but does not flower profusely every year. The flowers contrast well with the fresh green foliage.

'PINK STAR' (J. F. Letts, pre-1963) – June-Sept., 15 cm

Flowers clear mauve-pink, pointing horizontally all round; foliage grey-green; growth low and broad, rather lax.

A new cultivar, like the Dutch 'Helma', which bears 'star-shaped' horizontal flowers.

See plate 9.

Erica tetralix 'Lawsoniana' – See *E. mackaiana* 'Lawsoniana'

Erica tetralix 'Mackaiana' - See *E. mackaiana*

Erica tetralix 'Praegeri' – See *E.* × *praegeri*

ERICA UMBELLATA L. (1753)

English name: Portuguese Heath.

Distribution: Portugal, northern, western and southern Spain, North Africa (Morocco).

Description: A much-branched shrub of 20–60 (–90) cm. Leaves in whorls of 3. Flowers in umbels at the end of the shoots, globose, pink to red. Blooming April-June. Quite hardy.

ERICA VAGANS L. (1770)

English name: Cornish Heath.

Distribution: South-west England (Lizard, Cornwall), Western Ireland (Co. Fermanagh – where it is all white-flowered), western and central France, northern Portugal and northern Spain (see map on p. 85); naturalised in North America.

Description: An erect to spreading shrub 30 to 80 cm high. Leaves in whorls of 4 or 5, glabrous. Flowers bell-shaped, soft pink to purple-pink, in dense, many-flowered racemes up to 25 cm long. Blooming July-Oct (-Nov).

'ALBA' (1818) – July-Sept., 35 cm
Flowers white, with a slight pink tinge; foliage fresh green; growth broad erect.
Often confused with the creamy white 'Lyonesse'. In some nurseries they are mixed. The creamy-yellow colour of its stamens make it possible to distinguish this from the brownish-red of 'Alba'.

'GRANDIFLORA' (by 1868) – syn. 'Multiflora Grandiflora' – Aug-Oct., 75 cm
Flowers pale pink in very long racemes; growth vigorous, thin and tall.
This well known cultivar is often grown as 'Rosea'. The true 'Rosea' is pure soft pink and grows to only 40 cm high.

'HOLDEN PINK' (England, before 1960) – Aug-Sept., 30 cm*
Flowers light lilac-pink, in short, broad racemes; growth broad erect.
A very fine, free-flowering cultivar; a great improvement on the pale pink 'Carnea' and 'Pallida'.

'LYONESSE' (Maxwell & Beale, 1923) – July-Sept., 30 cm*
Flowers pure creamy white; foliage bright green; growth broad erect.
An exceptionally valuable form; an improvement on the very old 'Alba' (q.v.) which has a trace of pink.
'Kevernensis Alba' is slightly less tall; the flowers stand up in thin, lanky spikes. The colour is like that of 'Lyonesse'.

'MRS D. F. MAXWELL (Maxwell & Beale, by 1923) – Aug-Oct., 35 cm*
Flowers deep pinky red; foliage fresh green; growth rather dense and compact.

A very fine, widely grown cultivar.
The newer 'Diana Hornibrook' is almost identical; the colour
is slightly lighter (pinky red) and its flowers 2–3 weeks earlier.
See plate 12.

'NANA' (by 1879) – Aug-Oct., 20 (–30) cm
Flowers creamy white with striking red-brown anthers; foliage
delicate and yellowish green, particularly in winter; growth
very dense and squat.
A dwarf.

'PYRENEES PINK' (1931) – Aug-Oct., 35 cm*
Flowers pure salmon pink with red anthers, slightly darker
than 'St Keverne', later paler. A recommended cultivar.

'ST KEVERNE' syn. var *kevernensis* (1914) – Aug-Sept.,
35 cm*
Flowers pure salmon pink; foliage fresh green; growth rather
compact.
A beautiful, widely grown cultivar. Sometimes produces
shoots with lighter coloured flowers. When propagating, always be sure to take cuttings from shoots which have darker
flowers.

'VALERIE PROUDLEY' (Proudleys' Heather Nursery, 1968)
– Aug-Sept., 20 cm
Flowers white; foliage light golden-yellow; growth broad
erect. The first *E. vagans* with golden-yellow leaves. An attractive new plant.

Erica verticillata – See *E. manipuliflora*

Erica vulgaris – See *Calluna vulgaris*

Erica williamsiana – See *E.* × *williamsii*

Hybrids

ERICA × DARLEYENSIS Bean (1914)

Synonyms: E. mediterranea hybrida Hort.; *E. "hybrida"* Hort.; *E. "hybrida" darleyensis*
English name: Darley Dale Heath.
Origin: E. carnea × *E. erigena* (*E. mediterranea* Hort.).
Source: James Smith & Sons, Darley Dale, Derbyshire, England (around 1890).
A hybrid between *E. carnea* and *E. erigena.* The influence of the latter makes the growth more vigorous than that of *E. carnea.* The use of *E. erigena* in the cross also results in a slight loss of hardiness.
A number of cultivars are known. These include:

'DARLEY DALE' (J. Smith & Sons, *c.*1890) – Dec-May, 40 cm*
Flowers light purple-pink; foliage greyish green; growth broad erect, fairly vigorous, rather open.
This is the plant that has been grown under the name of plain *E.* × *darleyensis*; and in Germany as 'Böhlje'.

'GHOST HILLS' (J. H. Brummage, before 1962) – Jan-Apr., 40 cm*
Flowers bright purple-pink, later a very beautiful purple-red; growth broad erect.
A new cultivar that can be highly recommended; the colour is redder than that of the taller 'Arthur Johnson'.

'SILBERSCHMELZE' – syn. 'Molten Silver' (G. Arends, by 1937) – Nov-May, 40 cm*
Flowers silvery white; foliage greyish green, in winter dark bronze-green; growth like that of 'Darley Dale'.
An attractive hardy heath.
This has had many illegitimate synonyms, including 'Alba', 'Silver Beads', 'Silver Bells', 'Silver Flower', 'Silver Mist', 'Silver Star', 'Snow Flake' and 'White Form'.

'WHITE GLOW' (J. Drake, c.1955) – Jan-May, 40 cm
Flowers silvery white, like 'Silberschmelze' but slightly smaller; growth broad erect.
This is very little different from 'Silberschmelze'. It was introduced as a sport of E. carnea 'Ruby Glow'.

ERICA × PRAEGERI Ostenf. (1912)

Synonym: Erica tetralix 'Praegeri'
English name: Praeger's Heath.
Origin: E. mackaiana × E. tetralix.
Source: A natural hybrid, first found in Connemara, Ireland. Whether E. × praegeri is really a hybrid needs to be verified. It might possibly be a form of one or other parent.

'CONNEMARA' (1912) – July-Oct., 25 cm*
Flowers mauve-pink, freely produced; foliage dark green; growth broad erect, loose.
This is the clone that has been known for years under the name of plain E. × praegeri. A plant that can be recommended.
Some new forms with larger flowers found by Mr D. McClintock in Co Donegal in the North of Ireland are in cultivation as E. × praegeri 'Irish Lemon', 'Irish Orange' and 'Nacung'. The first two have particularly brightly coloured young growth.

117

ERICA 'STUARTII'

Synonym: E. tetralix ssp *stuartii* (Macf. 1893); *E.* × *stuartii* (Macf.) Linton (1902)
English name: Stuart's Heath.
Origin: A sport on *E.* × *praegeri.*
Source: Found in Connemara, Ireland (1890).
Flowers dark mauve-pink, pale at the base, with brown-black anthers, small; foliage dark green; growth up to 30 cm high with broad erect shoots.
An unusual plant on which, in Holland in 1977, a reversion to *E.* × *praegeri* was noticed, thus giving a clear indication of how it arose. It may therefore be termed *E.* × *praegeri* 'Stuartii'.

ERICA × VEITCHII Bean (1905)

English name: Veitch's Heath.
Origin: E. arborea × *E. lusitanica.*
Source: R. Veitch & Sons, Exeter, England (about 1895). A hybrid never noticed anywhere else.

'EXETER' (R. Veitch & Sons, *c.*1895) – Apr-May, 125 cm
Flowers white, in great masses on feather-shaped branches; growth erect.
This, the only clone, has been in cultivation as plain *E.* × *veitchii.* Quite hardy.
See plate 7.

ERICA × WATSONII (Benth.) Bean

Synonyms: E. ciliaris var. *watsonii* Benth. (1839).
E. mackaiana 'Watsonii', *E. "hybrida"* 'Watsonii'.
English name: Watson's Heath.
Origin: E. ciliaris × *E. tetralix.*
Source: A natural hybrid; first found by H. C. Watson near Truro, Cornwall, England (1832). The original clone is now called 'Truro'.

'DAWN' (Maxwell & Beale, 1925) – July-Oct., 25 cm*
Flowers mauve-pink; young shoots red in the spring, later golden, later still light green and finally dark green; growth very broad to erect.
A beautiful and free-flowering cultivar. Can be distinguished by its glandular hairs from 'H. Maxwell'.

'H. MAXWELL' (Maxwell & Beale, 1925) – July-Oct., 35 cm
Flowers bright mauve pink, plentiful; young shoots bronze-yellow to bronzy orange-red in the spring; growth broad to erect.
A fine, very free-flowering form. Can be distinguished from all other cultivars by the normal (not glandular) hairs.
See plate 12.

ERICA × WILLIAMSII Druce (1911)

Synonyms: E. vagans 'Williamsii'; *E. williamsiana* Hort.
English name: Williams' Heath.
Origin: E. tetralix × *E. vagans.*
Source: A natural hybrid, first collected by P. D. Williams near St Keverne, Cornwall, England (1910).

'P. D. WILLIAMS' (1910) – July-Oct., 20 cm

Flowers mauve-pink, in short racemes; foliage light green with golden young shoots, particularly in the spring; growth very broad.

Can be used for ground cover.

Has been generally known as plain *E.* × *williamsii*. Another cultivar, with pale mauve-pink flowers and more delicate yellow-green young shoots, is 'Gwavas'.

New and rare Calluna and Erica cultivars

Some information, briefly summarized, is given for heather enthusiasts and collectors about the following, mostly new, cultivars which have not been mentioned earlier.

	Flower Colour	Growth	Remarks
Calluna vulgaris			
'Alba Aurea'	pure white	spreading	tips yellow [1]
'Alba Carlton'	clear white	broad	foliage dark green
'Arina'	light purple	erect	
'Barbara Fleur'	pinky red	erect	
'Beoley Crimson'	purple-red	erect	
'Carole Chapman'	white	erect	foliage yellow
'Drum-Ra'	white	erect	
'E. Hoare'	purple-red	spreading	
'Firebreak'	pale purple	broad	tips red
'Foxhollow Wanderer'	purple	prostrate	
'Fred. J. Chapple'	purple-pink	erect	tips red [1]
'Fréjus'	light mauve	erect	very late [4]
'Grizzly'	purple-pink	erect	foliage grey-green
'Heidberg'	purple-pink	prostrate	foliage greyish
'Heideteppich'	purple	prostrate	flowers freely
'Hibernica'	purple-pink	broad	flowers freely
'Hollandia'	purple-pink	erect	late flowering
'Ingrid Bouter'	purple-red [3]	erect	flowers for a very long time
'Joy Vanstone'	light purple	erect	foliage yellow [2]
'Lyndon Proudley'	pink	compact	dwarf
'Mousehole'	purple-pink	compact	dwarf
'Mrs Alf'	light purple	spreading	tips red [1]
'Mrs Pat'	light mauve	broad	tips pink
'Pallida'	pale purple	erect	
'Petra'	light purple	very broad	flowers freely

1 in the spring; 2 changing colour in winter; 3 flowers double; 4 slightly tender

	Flower Colour	Growth	Remarks
'Prostrate Orange'	light purple	spreading	foliage yellow [2]
'Rannoch'	light purple	broad	foliage yellow [2]
'Roland Haagen'	light purple	erect	foliage yellow [2]
'Saint Nick'	purple-pink	spreading	flowers very late
'Sally-Anne Proudley'	light purple	erect	tips yellow [1] See plate 5.
'Silver Knight'	purple-pink	erect	foliage silver-grey
'Silver Rose'	purple-pink	erect	foliage silver-grey
'Silver Spire'	white	erect	foliage fresh green
'Spring Cream'	white	erect	foliage creamy yellow [1]
'Spring Torch'	light purple	erect	foliage red [1]
'Tom Thumb'	purple-pink	erect	dwarf
'Velvet Dome'	(purple)	very dense	dwarf
'Visser's Fancy'	lilac-purple	erect	late flowering
'White Gown'	clear white	erect	foliage grey-green
'Winter Chocolate'	purple-pink	broad	foliage yellow-green [2]

Erica carnea

'Alan Coates'	purple-pink	broad	foliage fresh green
'Alba'	white	very dense	small-flowered
'Anne Sparkes'	purple-red	broad	foliage / bronze-yellow
'December Red'	deep pink	broad	flowers freely
'Eileen Porter'	carmine pink	very dense	very early
'Foxhollow Fairy'	soft pink	spreading	
'Gracilis'	purple-pink	dense	early flowering
'March Seedling'	purple-pink	spreading	
'Pink Beauty'	pure pink	broad	free-flowering
'Pirbright Rose'	deep pink	spreading	
'R. B. Cooke'	bright pink	broad	vigorous
'Sherwoodii'	light pink	spreading	foliage soft green
'Vivellii Aurea'	purple red	broad	foliage bronze-yellow

Erica ciliaris

'Aurea'	mauve-pink	broad	foliage golden
'Maweana'	purple-pink	erect	late flowering
'Stapehill'	cream/purple	broad	
'Wych'	soft pink	broad	flowers freely

1 in the spring; 2 changing colour in winter;

	Flower Colour	Growth	Remarks
Erica cinerea			
'Alba Major'	pure white	erect	
'Ann Berry'	purple	erect	foliage yellow-green
'Apple Blossom'	pink-white	broad	
'Apricot Charm' (syn. 'Golden Heron')	mauve-pink	spreading	foliage yellow
'Atropurpurea'	deep purple	broad	
'Cairn Valley'	salmon pink	broad	flowers freely
'Colligan Bridge'	violet-purple	erect	foliage deep green
'Domino'	white	erect	calyx brown-red
'Eden Valley'	soft lilac	spreading	flowers freely
'England'	purple-lilac	erect	
'Frances'	salmon pink	erect	
'Glencairn'	pinky red	broad	tips red
'Golden Hue'	purple-pink	erect	foliage yellow. See plate 4.
'Guernsey Lime'	light purple	prostrate	foliage green-yellow
'Guernsey Pink'	pink	spreading	
'Guernsey Plum'	violet-purple	spreading	flowers freely
'Guernsey Purple'	light purple	spreading	
'Heidebrand'	deep red	broad	
'Honeymoon'	white (–lilac)	spreading	flowers freely
'Hookstone Lavender'	lavender-pink	erect	free-flowering
'Janet'	delicate pink	broad/low	foliage light green
'Lilacina'	light lilac	broad	
'Lilac Time'	soft lilac	erect	late-flowering
'My Love'	lilac-purple	spreading	flowers freely
'Old Rose'	light pink	spreading	
'Providence'	deep red	spreading	foliage deep green
'Purple Beauty'	violet-purple	spreading	
'Rock Pool' (syn 'Golden Grass')	purple	spreading	foliage deep yellow
'Rose Queen'	salmon pink	erect	flowers freely
'Sea Foam'	mauve-white	spreading	
'Violetta'	violet-purple	erect	flowers freely
'Vivienne Patricia'	mauve-lilac	erect	flowers freely
Erica × darleyensis			
'Erecta'	purple-pink	erect	
'Furzey'	purple-pink	erect	flowers freely
'George Rendall'	purple-pink	spreading	

	Flower Colour	*Growth*	*Remarks*
'Jack H. Brummage'	purple-pink	broad	foliage light yellow [1]
'J. W. Porter'	purple-red	erect	foliage pink/yellow [1]
'Margaret Porter'	light pink	erect	
'Darleyensis'	salmon pink	spreading	
'Mary Grace'	soft pink	erect	corolla usually split
'Pink Glow'	bright pink	erect	foliage grey
'Silver Bells'	white with pink	broad	foliage green
'Tina'	pinky red	broad	foliage grey

Erica vagans

'Birch Glow'	pinky red	broad	
'Cream'	creamy white	erect	
'Hookstone Rose'	salmon pink	erect	foliage deep green
'Rubra'	purple-red	broad/loose	
'Summertime'	salmon pink	broad	
'Viridiflora'	(light pink)	erect	most flowers distorted green by mites
'White Rocket'	white	erect	

Erica × watsonii

'F. White'	white with pink	broad	flowers for a long time
'Gwen'	light pink	broad	
'Rachel'	mauve-pink	broad	foliage deep green

1 in the spring

Flowering calendar for some Callunas and Ericas

SPECIES AND CULTIVARS	Jan	Feb	Mar	Apr	May	Jun	Jul	Aug	Sep	Oct	Nov	Dec
E. carnea												
'Praecox Rubra'	■	■	■									
E. × darleyensis												
'Silberschmelze'	■	■	■	■	■							
'Darley Dale'	■	■	■	■								
'Ghost Hills'												■
E. carnea												
'King George'	■	■	■									
'Snow Queen'	■	■	■									■
'Aurea'		■	■									
'Pink Spangles'		■	■	■								
'Ruby Glow'		■	■	■								
'Springwood Pink'		■	■	■								
'Springwood White'			■	■								
'Heathwood'			■	■								
'James Backhouse'			■	■								
'Loughrigg'			■	■								
'Myretoun Ruby'			■	■								
'Vivellii'			■	■								
E. arborea												
'Alpina'				■	■							
E. erigena												
'W. T. Rackliff'				■	■							
E. cinerea												
'Alba Minor'						■	■	■	■	■		
'C. D. Eason'						■	■	■	■			
'Coccinea'						■	■	■	■			
'Katinka'						■	■	■	■			
'Pallas'						■	■	■	■	■		
'Pink Ice'						■	■	■	■			
'Rosea'						■	■	■	■			
E. tetralix												
'Alba' / 'Alba Mollis'						■	■	■	■	■		
'Hookstone Pink'						■	■	■	■	■		
'Ken Underwood'						■	■	■	■	■		
C. vulgaris												
'Alba Praecox'						■	■	■	■			
'Tenuis'						■	■	■	■	■		
'Tib'						■	■	■	■			
E. mackaiana												
'Wm M'Alla'							■	■	■			

SPECIES AND CULTIVARS	Jan	Feb	Mar	Apr	May	Jun	Jul	Aug	Sep	Oct	Nov	Dec
E. tetralix												
'Con Underwood'								▓	▓			
'Helma'								▓	▓			
E. vagans												
'Lyonesse'								▓	▓			
E. ciliaris												
'Globosa'								▓	▓	▓		
E. cinerea												
'Atrosanguinea'/							▓	▓	▓			
Smith's Variety												
E. × *praegeri*												
'Connemara'							▓	▓	▓			
E. terminalis							▓	▓	▓			
E. × *watsonii*												
'Dawn'							▓	▓	▓			
'H. Maxwell'							▓	▓	▓			
E. × *williamsii*												
'P. D. Williams'							▓	▓	▓			
E. cinerea												
'G. Osmond'							▓	▓	▓			
'Grandiflora'							▓	▓	▓			
f. *schizopetala*							▓	▓	▓			
'Stephen Davis'							▓	▓	▓			
C. vulgaris												
'Foxii Nana'						▓						
E. cinerea												
'Alba'								▓	▓			
'Cevennes'								▓	▓			
'C. G. Best'								▓	▓			
'P. S. Patrick'								▓	▓			
C. vulgaris												
'Alba Erecta'								▓	▓			
'Barnett Anley'								▓	▓			
'Beoley Gold'								▓	▓			
'County Wicklow'								▓	▓			
'Cuprea'								▓	▓			
'C. W. Nix'								▓	▓			
'Darkness'								▓	▓			
'Darleyensis'								▓	▓			
'Elegantissima'								▓	▓			
'J. H. Hamilton'								▓	▓			
'Mullion'								▓	▓			
'Nana Compacta'								▓	▓			

SPECIES AND CULTIVARS	Jan	Feb	Mar	Apr	May	Jun	Jul	Aug	Sep	Oct	Nov	Dec
'Radnor'								■	■			
'Silver Queen'								■	■			
'Alba Plena'								■	■	■		
'Mrs Ronald Gray'								■	■	■		
E. vagans												
'Grandiflora'								■	■			
'Mrs D. F. Maxwell'								■	■			
'St Keverne'								■	■			
C. vulgaris												
'Elsie Purnell'									■	■		
'H. E. Beale'									■	■		
'Long White'									■	■		
'Peter Sparkes'									■	■		
'Serlei'									■	■		
'David Eason'									■	■	■	
'Battle of Arnhem'										■	■	■

Other members of the Erica family

It could be said, paradoxically, that a heather garden is not a proper heather garden if it does not also contain other plants which, like *Calluna* and *Erica*, belong to the Ericaceae (the heather family). This view should not be brushed aside lightly; there are too many fine plants in this family that combine exceptionally well with heathers. Some have spectacular flower colours (*Kalmia* and *Rhododendron*); others owe their ornamental value to the colour of their leaves (*Pieris*, *Zenobia*), their fruits (*Gaultheria*, *Pernettya*) or their particular habit of growth (*Arctostaphylos*). The fascination of other species lies in the mass of small flowers (*Cassiope*, *Daboecia*); or the brilliant colour of their leaves in autumn may be a wonderful sight (*Enkianthus*).

Of course one must be careful not to plant, for instance, too many vivid red rhododendrons, although these mostly flower in a period when there are not many heathers in flower. Very early flowering rhododendrons such as 'Christmas Cheer', 'Praecox' and 'Tessa' might distract attention from heathers which recently have been pruned and may therefore be temporarily looking unattractive.

Tastes differ, and there is no accounting for tastes; everyone plants his garden in his own way. If we watch and listen to what other people do and say, we can expect to learn something, and we shall certainly come to understand better the art of grouping plants. '*Experientia docet*' is very true.

I hope a happy choice can be made from the following very short list:

A mixture of *Calluna* and *Erica*

A garden with *Erica cinerea* 'Golden Hue'

landscaped garden

A heather garden with ivy (*Hedera*)

12 *Erica* × *watsonii* 'H. Maxwell'

Erica tetralix 'Ardy'

Erica vagans 'Mrs. D. F. Maxwell'

Daboecia cantabrica 'Praegerae'

Cassiope 'Muirhead'

Kalmia polifolia

Andromeda polifolia (Bog Rosemary)

A small shrub with procumbent to erect shoots; the leaves are
narrow, leathery and glossy green; flowers pink, in drooping
racemes, May-June.

Bog Rosemary will only grow on peaty and moisture-
holding soils. *A. polifolia* 'Compacta' is a low-growing form.
'Nikko' and 'Shibutsu' are very fine new cultivars from Japan.
Another species is *A. glaucophylla*. Its cv. 'Latifolia' has broader
leaves.

Arctostaphylos uva-ursi (Bearberry)

A prostrate shrublet with glossy green leaves on red-brown
stems; flowers in April-June, white or white-pink, in racemes
of 3 to 12; fruits berry-like, globular, scarlet-red.

Bearberry tolerates a fairly dry soil and a position in full
sun. If the rooting shoots are not disturbed, a single specimen
can in time cover a considerable area. The new 'Rax' has
a very compact habit. Plants coming from the continent as
A. nevadensis are nearly all *A. uva-ursi*. *Arctostaphylos* can be
propagated by seed, cuttings or layers.

Bruckenthalia spiculifolia (Balkan Heath)

A heather-like shrublet with small needle-shaped leaves; flowers small, bright pink, in short dense racemes, June (–September). A dwarf that can be highly recommended for small
gardens.

Cassiope

This genus contains about 12 species and several varieties and
hybrids. Most of the species are found in the northern part of
the northern hemisphere, even as far as Alaska. Others are
known from the Himalayas.

They are low-growing, evergreen shrubs with a mass of small white or sometimes pale pink bells in April-May. They prefer a rather acid soil, rich in humus, and a position in light shade.

Cassiope is unfortunately not very often grown. Some beautiful species are: *C. lycopodioides, C. mertensiana, C. selaginoides, C. tetragona* and *C. wardii*. The hybrids 'Edinburgh' and 'Muirhead' are also valuable (see plate 12).

Chamaedaphne calyculata (syn. *Andromeda calyculata*)
(Leather-leaf)

A small evergreen shrub; leaves with brown scales on both sides, shoots pendulous; flowers white, March-April.

A low-growing form with horizontal branches is 'Nana'.

Daboecia cantabrica (St Dabeoc's Heath)

A low, evergreen Irish native with broad fresh green leaves, silvery beneath, and urn-shaped flowers in long terminal racemes, from June sometimes into December.

In very cold areas *Daboecia* can suffer from frost; f. *alba*, covers all white forms.

'Atropurpurea', flowers deep purple-pink; growth vigorous.

'Bicolor', flowers purple, white or white with purple stripes on the same shoot. (See p. 73)

'Cinderella', flowers very pale pinky-white.

'Globosa Pink', flowers purple-pink, globose; growth wide.

'Praegerae', flowers a bright deep pink; growth spreading with erect shoots. Perhaps the most susceptible to severe frost. (See plate 12).

'Purpurea', flowers bright purple-pink.

'William Buchanan' is a form of *Daboecia azorica* × *D. can-*

tabrica (D. × scotica): flowers a vivid crimson, small, in great profusion, from June to October. Very valuable.

Enkianthus campanulatus

A broad, erect shrub with leaves 3–7 cm long; flowers urn-shaped, pink, striped, in pendulous racemes, May. Fine autumn colour.

Gaultheria procumbens (Creeping Wintergreen. Checkerberry)

A very low, creeping, evergreen shrub with almost round leaves, 1½–3 cm in diameter; flowers in July and August, white or white-pink, not very conspicuous; fruits berry-shaped, bright red.

A slightly taller June-flowering species with white 'berries' is *G. miqueliana*.

G. shallon grows to 1 m high, has oval leaves 5–12 cm long and purple-black 'berries' and forms thickets in some places.

Kalmia angustifolia (Sheep Laurel)

A narrow, erect, small, evergreen shrub with lanceolate leaves; naturalised in two or three places in Britain, flowers 1 cm in diameter, dark pink, in clusters, June-July. 'Rubra' is a beautiful selection with blue-green leaves and wine-red flowers. This flowers over a long period.

K. latifolia (Calico Bush) is a vigorous bush with leaves 7–12 cm long and pink flowers 2–3 cm in diameter.

K. polifolia (K. glauca), a particularly beautiful plant for the heather garden, is naturalised in Surrey. It has narrow, light green leaves and pure pink flowers in terminal umbels. April-May. (See plate 12.).

Kalmias should be planted on a well-drained site and prefer light shade. The species are usually raised from seed.

Ledum groenlandicum (syn. *L. latifolium*) (Labrador Tea)

A small evergreen shrub naturalised in the north of the British Isles, up to about 1 m high with shoots covered in brown felt and leaves 2–5 cm long, rusty brown and tomentose on the lower side; the young leaves particularly have an aromatic smell. The white flowers are clustered in umbels 5 cm wide. Blooms May-June.

'Compactum' is better known than the species and also more suitable for heather gardens, having a much squatter habit, smaller leaves and narrower umbels.

L. palustre and *L. glandulosum* are beautiful but very difficult to get hold of. All the species like a moist situation.

Leucothoë fontanesiana (syn. *L. catesbaei; Andromeda catesbaei*)

A shrub with pendulous shoots that keeps its leaves throughout the year; leaves narrow, 8–12 cm, long pointed, arranged in 2 rows, deep bronze in winter; flowers white, in racemes, May-June.

Should only be planted in large gardens. Tolerates shade well.

Pernettya mucronata

A hardy, dioecious, evergreen, suckering shrub with sharp-pointed, glossy, dark green leaves, naturalised in Britain. The 10–16 mm-wide berries vary in colour from white, lilac, pink and crimson to deep red.

To ensure fruiting, male specimens must also be planted. It is best to place these on the south-west side of the berry-bearing plants, because they are wind-pollinated.

Phyllodoce

Exceptionally fine small evergreen shrubs with procumbent to ascending shoots; leaves linear, 6–15 mm long; flowers in racemes or umbels, April-June.

These plants, which are not seen very often, prefer a moist, well-drained soil, rich in humus, and a lightly shaded position.

Phyllodoce can be propagated by seed, layers or cuttings. Some good species are: *P. aleutica* (creamy white), *P. breweri* (purple-pink), *P. caerulea* (*P. taxifolia*) (a Scottish native, blue-purple) and *P. empetriformis*. A fine hybrid is *P. × intermedia* 'Fred Stoker'.

Pieris japonica (syn. *Andromeda japonica*)

An evergreen shrub, rather slow growing, with glossy green leaves; flowers in pendulous panicles, white, March-April.

'Select' is an excellent, free-flowering form. The white-marked 'Variegata' is also worth planting.

P. formosa var. *forrestii (P. forrestii)* makes much stouter growth. The colour of the young leaves is a brilliant red. 'Wakehurst' is particularly well worth having.

'Forest Flame' is a hybrid of *P. formosa* var. *forrestii* 'Wakehurst' and *P. japonica*. Its young leaves are just as finely coloured. An exceptionally good plant for the heather garden.

P. floribunda is very hardy. This moderately tall shrub has erect panicles during March-April.

The species and the var. *forrestii* can be raised from seeds.

Rhododendron (including *Azalea*)

This genus has such an abundance of forms that a separate book could be written about it. Many may be planted with heathers. Obviously only a limited number can be referred to here. Since there are so many small heather gardens, we

133

shall choose mainly from among the dwarf rhododendrons.

Like most of the Ericaceae, rhododendrons grow best in moist soils, rich in humus. To protect the soil from direct sun, it is advisable to spread a thin layer of woodland soil or garden peat around the plants after planting. Removing the dead flower trusses immediately improves growth and bud formation.

SPECIES

camtschaticum, purple-pink, May-June; 20 cm; deciduous.
ferrugineum (Alpine Rose), pink-red, June-July; 30 cm
hirsutum (Alpine Rose), bright pink, June-July; 40 cm
impeditum, lilac-blue, April-May; 40 cm
racemosum, soft pink, March-May; 60 cm
russatum (syn. *cantabile*), dark violet, April-May; 60 cm
williamsianum, light pink, April-May; 80 cm
yakusimanum, pink to white, May-June; 50 cm

DWARF HYBRIDS (pinky-white to violet-blue)
'Blue Diamond', bright violet-blue, April-May; 80 cm
'Blue Tit', light lavender-blue, April-May; 80 cm
'Christmas Cheer', pinkish-white, February-March; 80 cm
'Moerheim', lilac-purple, April; 30 cm
'Praecox', clear pinkish-purple, February-April; 150 cm
'Tessa', clear lilac-pink, February-March; 150 cm

REPENS HYBRIDS (red)
'Baden-Baden', scarlet-red, May; 80 cm
'Elizabeth', salmon red, April; 80 cm
'Scarlet Wonder', bright red, April-May; 60 cm

WILLIAMSIANUM HYBRIDS (pink)
'Karin', pure deep pink, frilled, April-May; 80 cm
'Linda', bright pink-red, May; 80 cm

HYBRIDS for larger gardens
'America', bright red, May; 200 cm
'Blue Peter', light lavender-blue, May; 125 cm
'Catawbiense Grandiflorum', lilac, May-June; 250 cm
'Cunningham's White', white, April-May; 200 cm
'Pink Pearl', light pink, May; 200 cm
'Roseum Elegans', pink-lilac, May; 200 cm

JAPANESE AZALEAS
'Amoena', clear lilac-purple, very small, May; 60 cm
'Campfire', deep red, May; 80 cm
'Favorite', pure deep pink, May; 80 cm
'Hatsugiri', lilac-purple, small, May; 40 cm
'Hino-crimson', deep crimson, April; 60 cm
'Silvester', pink, dark centre, small, April; 40 cm

Vaccinium vitis-idaea (Cowberry)
A low-growing, evergreen shrub up to 25 cm high; leaves
leathery, $1\frac{1}{2}$–$2\frac{1}{2}$ cm long, dark green; fruits berry-shaped, in
small racemes, red, September-November.
    'Koralle' is a cultivar with abundant large fruits.
    V. macrocarpon (syn. *Oxycoccus macrocarpos*), American Cran-
berry is a mat-forming, prostrate little plant with very long,
thin shoots and 8–15 mm-long leaves. The small pink flowers
develop into red berries $1\frac{1}{2}$–2 cm large. In America certain
large-fruited forms are grown on a very large scale; the fruits
are picked for cranberry sauce. Jam, soft drinks and also wine
are made from them.
    V. myrtillus is our native Bilberry (Blaeberry, Whortleberry,
Whinberry or Hurts). In a large garden it would be quite
acceptable to plant one or more bushes of the large-fruited
Highbush Blueberry (*V. corymbosum*) that comes from America. There are several valuable cultivars of this.

Zenobia pulverulenta (syn. *Zenobia speciosa; Andromeda pulverulenta*)

A semi-evergreen little shrub up to about 1 m high; leaves 4–6 cm, thickly covered with a blue-white bloom which gradually wears off as the season advances; flowers in clusters, white, May-June.

The var. *viridis* (syn. var. *nuda*; var. *nitida*) has no bloom on the shoots and leaves. Both the species and the variety can be recommended for the heather garden.

In addition to the above-mentioned plants, there are a number of other members of the Ericaceae that it would be interesting to plant among heathers. They are not readily enough obtainable, however, to justify describing them in this little book.

These scarcer members of the Ericaceae include: *Arctous alpinus* (Alpine Bearberry, a Scottish native), *Epigaea repens, Gaulnettya × wisleyensis* 'Wisley Pearl', *Gaylussacia dumosa, Leiophyllum buxifolium, Loiseleuria procumbens* (Alpine Azalea, another Scottish native), *Lyonia ligustrina, Menziesia ciliicalyx, Oxydendrum arboreum, Rhodothamnus chamaecistus* and *Tripetaleia bracteata*.

Other ornamental shrubs

In addition to the 'Other members of the Ericaceae', there are many fine small shrubs or even trees that go well with heathers. Some of them, indeed, are indispensable. Thus the picturesque white stems of birch (*Betula*) should certainly not be missing from large plantings. The various species of broom (*Cytisus* and *Genista*), too, and gorse (*Ulex*) can be highly recommended, especially for reasonably large gardens.

In fact, a relatively wide range of woody plants can be used in a heather garden, provided one takes into account the structure of the plants. Thus the finely branched common broom (*Cytisus scoparius*) fits very well among heathers, whereas large-leaved bushes or trees such as *Magnolia* × *soulangeana* or the tulip tree (*Liriodendron tulipifera*) must be avoided.

Perhaps a choice could be made from among the following:

Acer palmatum 'Dissectum' (Japanese Maple)
A small shrub with very deeply divided, fresh green leaves. 'Dissectum Nigrum' has deep purple-brown foliage. Both have fine autumn colour and are dwarf maples.

Amelanchier lamarckii (syn. *A.* × *grandiflora*) (Snowy Mespilus)
A robust bush or small tree with racemes of white flowers in April-May, currant-like fruits and vivid red autumn colour; naturalised in N.W. Europe including England. Often grown as *A. canadensis*, but also mis-called *A. laevis* f. *villosa* or *A. confusa*.

Betula nana (Dwarf Birch)
A small British native shrub with nearly round, dark green leaves.

B. pendula (syn. *B. alba; B. verrucosa*) (Silver Birch)
A vigorous native tree with a conspicuously white trunk. For larger gardens.

Cytisus scoparius (syn. *Sarothamnus scoparius*) (Broom)
A native with thin green shoots and abundant yellow flowers. For dry soils. *C.* × *praecox* (creamy yellow) and *C.* 'Hollandia' (purple-red) are also suitable. *C. purpureus* 'Atropurpureus' is a low broom with a broad habit and dark purple-pink flowers.

Empetrum nigrum (Crowberry)
A creeping, heather-like native with dark green foliage, minute flowers and large black berries. A dioecious plant (see the note on *Pernettya*, p. 132).
Very suitable for the heather garden. Prefers acid, moist soil; grows even in shade.

Genista anglica (Petty Whin)
A procumbent to erect, thorny little native with yellow flowers. Thrives on dry, poor, sandy soils. Blooms June-July.
Other species of *Genista* are: *G. germanica, G. hispanica* (Spanish Gorse), *G. lydia, G. pilosa* (Hairy Greenweed, a rare native), *G. sagittalis, G. sylvestris* var. *pungens* (*G. dalmatica*) and *G. tinctoria* (Dyer's Greenweed, another native).
Of this latter species, the prostrate var. *humifusa* and the var. *litoralis* can be particularly recommended.

Hebe ochracea (syn. *H. armstrongii* Hort.; *Veronica armstrongii*)
A much branched, conifer-like small shrub with bronze-coloured 'whipcord' foliage. Flowers in July-August, white.
The genus *Hebe* is closely related to *Veronica* (Speedwell); many species are known. The green-leaved *H. buxifolia* and the blue-grey-leaved *H. pinguifolia* 'Pagei' make an attractive combination.

Ilex crenata 'Convexa'
A small evergreen shrub with convex, fresh green leaves; fruits black.

138

Lavandula angustifolia (syn. *L. spica*) (Lavender)
An erect, aromatic small shrub with grey-green, linear leaves.
Flowers lavender-blue, July-August.

'Hidcote', 'Middactcn' and 'Munstead' are valuable cultivars.

Myrica gale (Bog Myrtle)
A small, deciduous aromatic native with decorative catkins
in March-April.

Suitable at the edge of a lake or bog, more or less in the
water.

Potentilla 'Elizabeth' (syn. *P. fruticosa* 'Arbuscula' Hort.)
(*P. arbuscula* × *P. fruticosa*)
A low and broad shrub up to 100 cm high, with grey-green
foliage and large pale yellow flowers from June onwards.

P. fruticosa 'Primrose Beauty' is only half as high with
spreading shoots, blue-grey foliage and creamy yellow flowers.

Salix helvetica (Swiss Willow)
A small shrub with striking silver-grey leaves and pretty catkins.

S. repens var. *argentea* (*nitida, arenaria*) is a native silver-leaved
variety of the Creeping Willow. *S. exigua* (Coyote Willow) is a
taller species with very narrow, grey-white leaves.

Santolina chamaecyparissus (Lavender Cotton)
A small, evergreen, strongly aromatic shrub, covered with
grey felt; flowers yellow, July-August.

Ulex europaeus (Gorse)
A well-known prickly native with green twigs and pure yellow
flowers at their finest from March to May.

The double-flowered 'Plenus' is sterile, and so flowers over a
long period.

The following low-growing plants are often looked on as herbaceous perennials but are in fact woody.

Dryas octopetala (Mountain Avens)
A small procumbent native with leaves with rounded teeth; flowers large, white, usually with 8 petals, May-June; fruits with long feathery grey styles.
   D. × *suendermanii* is an attractive hybrid.

Helianthemum (Rock Rose)
Small shrubs with beautiful flowers (in sunny weather) in a variety of colours. The grey-leaved hybrids are particularly suitable for the heather garden. These include: 'Ben Fhada' (golden with an orange centre), 'Ben Hope' (carmine pink with a deep orange centre) and 'The Bride' (creamy white with a yellow centre).

Hypericum olympicum (St John's Wort)
A low, broad little plant with stems woody at the base, small, blue-grey leaves and 3–4 cm golden flowers.

Thymus (Thyme)
Very low, often creeping little shrubs with greyish foliage and small, lilac-pink, purple-lilac or white flowers. They are excellent ground cover plants. Sometimes they make very rampant growth.
   T. praecox (*T. "serpyllum"*, incl. *T. drucei* and *T. lanuginosus*) and *T. pulegioides* can be recommended. Both are British.

Conifers

Conifers are undoubtedly the most important plants for embellishing, or perhaps it is better to say furnishing, heather gardens. They add a certain distinction that can be given by few other plants.

Generally the non-specialist goes first for the strikingly coloured ones, so that his garden gives a spotty and unrestful impression. With all the fine foliage colours in the heathers, it is unnecessary for the conifers to have blue, and particularly yellow, tones as well. Some people think that all strikingly yellow and blue conifers should be kept out of the heather garden. One can, of course, understand this point of view.

The range of conifers is incredibly large. Many books have been written about them, and it is difficult to make the right choice. Those that are mentioned here are only a handful. They are mostly dwarfs, which are particularly suitable for the smaller heather gardens that are now the most usual.

Abies balsamea 'Hudsonia' (Syn. 'Nana')
A small dwarf form with dense, flattened-spherical growth; needles short, dark green.

A. koreana
A broad pyramidal, small tree with bright green needles, conspicuously white on the lower side; cones usually purple-blue, freely borne. One of the most beautiful little conifers for the heather garden; bears cones at an early age.

Chamaecyparis lawsoniana 'Columnaris' ('Columnaris Glauca')
A fairly vigorous columnar form with deep blue-green foliage, rather resembling 'Allumii'. 'Golden Wonder', 'Lanei' and 'Stewartii' are fine plants with yellow foliage. All are suitable for the larger heather garden and are widely grown.

'Ellwoodii'
A dense, fairly small, columnar plant of a grey-green colour. Very widely grown. 'Chilworth Silver' is an improvement with blue-grey foliage. Both are juvenile forms. 'Minima Glauca' is a dwarf with a rounded growth habit.

C. obtusa 'Crippsii'
A broad pyramidal, rather slow-growing, elegant tree with beautiful golden foliage. An exceptionally good plant for the heather garden. 'Tetragona Aurea', which also has golden leaves, is interesting too.

'Nana Gracilis'
A strange dwarf with fresh green foliage. One of the best known dwarf conifers. Highly recommended.

C. pisifera 'Boulevard'
A dense form with a broad pyramidal habit; foliage exceptionally grey-blue, changing colour very little in winter. Very fine; older leaves often turn brown.

'Filifera Aurea'
A slow-growing, rather rounded plant with golden, pendulous, thread-like shoots.

'Plumosa Rogersii'
A plant up to 1 m high with a broad, conical habit; leaves needle-shaped (juvenile form), golden, even in winter.

Cryptomeria japonica 'Globosa Nana'
A dwarf with a dense, rounded habit; foliage light green, in winter somewhat blue-green.

'Jindai-Sugi'
Also a dwarf with a curious habit; needles light green, even in winter.

'Vilmoriniana'
A very slow-growing dwarf with a nearly globular, dense habit; foliage green, in winter somewhat purple-brown. A cultivar that can be recommended.

Juniperus communis 'Hibernica'
This is the finest columnar form among the junipers; it lends a special distinction to a heather garden. It should not be absent from any planting of heathers.

'Pyramidalis' ('Suecica') is another erect form; 'Compressa' a dwarf among the erect cultivars.

'Repanda'
A broad plant found in Ireland with spreading branches, eventually reaching 60 cm high, foliage green. A fine form that is widely grown.

'Hornibrookii' is another Irish form, with prostrate branches.

J. horizontalis 'Wiltonii' (syn. 'Glauca', 'Blue Rug')
A plant that spreads out flat over the ground, with grey-blue foliage. A very beautiful ground-cover plant for larger areas; indeed, it is sometimes planted instead of grass.

J. × *media*
A group of conifers that are still often called *J. chinensis*. The best cultivars for the heather garden are:

'Blaauw'
Growth fairly dense, rather spreading; foliage blue-green. A very fine form; 'Plumosa Aurea' is somewhat similar with bronze-yellow foliage and more vigorous growth.

'Old Gold'
Habit broad, spreading; more compact than 'Pfitzeriana Aurea'; foliage golden. Suitable for the larger garden.

J. squamata 'Blue Star'
An exceptionally compact, elegant plant, with an irregular, more or less rounded habit; foliage silvery blue. Recommended for the small garden.

J. virginiana 'Skyrocket'
A particularly slender, columnar form with blue-grey foliage. Grows erect and very fast. Particularly suitable for the medium-sized heather garden. 'Canaertii' and 'Glauca' are cultivars for larger gardens.

Picea abies
This is the well-known Christmas tree. There are very many slow-growing cultivars for the small to medium-sized garden. Some of these are:

'Gregoryana'
A very dense plant with a nearly globular habit; needles green. The still fairly new 'Little Gem' also grows exceptionally slowly. The well-known 'Ohlendorffii' grows more vigorously.

'Inversa'
A curious plant with shoots that are erect, pendulous or even prostrate over the ground; does not form a single head.

'Nidiformis'
Broad, spreading growth and green needles. 'Repens' grows even lower and very wide. See plate 6.

P. glauca var. *albertiana* 'Conica'
A well known form that grows slowly and has a dense, broad pyramidal habit; needles green to rather grey-green.

'Echiniformis' is a true dwarf with globular very dense growth and blue-green foliage.

144

P. omorika

The well known Serbian **Spruce** with slender growth and elegant drooping branches. Only to be used in large gardens.

'Nana' is a dwarf with a flattened spherical habit.

P. orientalis

A broad pyramidal, fairly large tree with short, dark green needles. Suitable for larger gardens.

P. pungens 'Globosa' (Syn. 'Glauca Globosa')

A dwarf among the blue spruces, with a rather dense, irregularly rounded growth habit; needles very short, a striking blue-grey.

'Procumbens' ('Glauca Procumbens') is a rare but very beautiful prostrate form. For large gardens the erect cultivars like 'Koster' and 'Moerheimii' can be recommended.

Pinus mugo var. *mughus*

The Mountain Pine with a fairly dense growth habit and green needles.

Is raised from seed and is very variable in growth.

The var. *pumilio* has a lower, more prostrate and compact growth habit.

P. parviflora

An elegant, fairly vigorous tree with twisted, blue-grey needles. Recommended for larger gardens.

P. pumila

A dwarf form of broad, bushy growth; needles thin, blue-green, useful in small gardens.

P. pumila 'Watereri' (syn. 'Pumila')

A broad, fairly dense, slow-growing shrub with conspicuously grey-green needles. Highly recommended for small to medium-sized gardens.

Taxus baccata 'Fastigiata' (Irish Yew, Florence Court Yew)
A columnar conifer with dark green needles. The golden-variegated form is called 'Fastigiata Aureomarginata', often grown as 'Fastigiata Aurea'.

'Repandens'
A very broad and low plant with dark green needles.
For gardens of considerable dimensions 'Semperaurea' with yellower leaves, can be used. *T. cuspidata* 'Nana' is also particularly suitable for these.

Thuja occidentalis 'Rheingold'
A dwarf form that is sometimes nearly spherical, with irregular growth and an unusual colour that turns orange-brown in winter. A fine cultivar.

T. orientalis 'Aurea Nana'
One of the most beautiful dwarf conifers with a dense, oval habit and strikingly yellow foliage, even in winter.
    For somewhat larger gardens the more erect 'Elegantissima', that turns orange-brown in winter, is very suitable.

Tsuga canadensis 'Nana'
A compact, flattened spherical dwarf with fresh green needles.
    The older 'Pendula' is a weeping form.

Glossary

anther, the part of a stamen that contains the pollen.

bract, leaves, usually small, in an inflorescence.

calyx, the outermost, usually green, whorl of a perianth.

ciliate, fringed with hairs.

corolla, the innermost, usually coloured, whorl of a perianth.

decussate, successive pairs of leaves at right angles to each other.

dioecious, male and female flowers on different plants.

double, a flower with more, or many more, petals than normal.

glabrous, without hairs.

gland, a superficial secretory organ, often shining.

inflorescence, a flowering shoot.

male, a flower that has stamens but no pistil.

ovary, the base of the style enclosing the embryo seeds.

ovoid, egg-shaped.

panicle, a branched raceme.

perianth, the floral envelope.

pistil, the female organ of a flower.

procumbent, lying along the ground.

raceme, an unbranched inflorescence with stalked flowers along the axis.

sepal, a segment of the calyx.

stamen, the male organ in a flower that produces pollen.

sterile, unfruitful, producing no pollen or seed.

stigma, the receptive, usually topmost, generally broadened, part of a pistil.

style, the narrow part of the pistil above the ovary and below the stigma.

tomentose, with a dense, matted, soft covering of hairs.

umbel, an inflorescence with a number of stalked flowers arising from a common point.

Meaning of scientific epithets

The generic epithets used in this book are given below in the masculine form (usually with the –*us* ending), although nearly all trees and shrubs – including heathers – are feminine, their epithets usually with an –*a* ending. The list excludes epithets named after people.

affinis, related
albus, white
aleuticus, of the Aleutian Islands
alpinus, from alpine regions
anglicus, English
angustifolius, narrow-leaved
arboreus, tree-like
arbusculus, like a small tree
arenarius, sandy places
argenteus, silver-white
atropurpureus, dark purple
atrorubens, atroruber, dark red
atrosanguineus, dark blood red
aureus, golden, gold-coloured
australis, from the south
azoricus, from the Azores

bicolor, two-coloured
borealis, northern
brachysepalus, with short sepals
bracteatus, with bracts
buxifolius, with Box-like leaves
caeruleus, dark blue
calyculatus, with an outer calyx
campanulatus, bell-shaped

camtschaticus, of Kamchatka
cantabilis, worthy of a song
cantabricus, from the Cantabrian
    Mountains, N. Spain
carneus, flesh pink
chamaecistus, dwarf cistus
chamaecyparissus, dwarf Cypress
ciliaris, having eye-lashes, i.e. hairs
    at the edge
ciliicalyx, with a ciliate calyx
cinereus, ash grey
coccineus, carmine red, scarlet red
codonodes, bell-like
columnaris, column-shaped
communis, usual, common
compactus, compact
compressus, compressed, flat
confusus, confused
conicus, conical
corsicus, Corsican
corymbosus, with flowers in corymbs
crenatus, with rounded teeth
cupreus, copper-coloured

dalmaticus, of Dalmatia

dissectus, deeply indented
dumosus, bushy

echiniformis, prickle-shaped
elegans, elegant
elegantissimus, most elegant
empetriformis, crowberry-like
erectus, erect, straight
erigenus, early born (intended to
    mean of Irish origin)
europaeus, European
exiguus, little

fastigiatus, branches erect and
    parallel
ferrugineus, rust-coloured
filiferus, bearing threads
flagelliformis, whip-shaped
flore pleno, with double flowers
floribundus, free-flowering
formosus, handsome
fruticosus, bushy, shrubby
fulgidus, shining, bright-coloured

gale, from the English 'Sweet Gale'
genuina, genuine
germanicus, German
glaber, smooth, bare, hairless
glandulosus, with glands
glaucus, blue-green, sea-green
globosus, spherical
grandiflorus, large-flowered
groenlandicus, of Greenland

helveticus, Swiss
herbaceus, herbaceous, grass-green
    coloured

hibernicus, Irish, or winter-flowering
hirsutus, hairy
hispanicus, Spanish
humifusus, procumbent
hybridus, mixed, intermediate

impeditus, hindered
incanus, grey, hoary
intermedius, intermediate
inversus, upside-down

japonicus, Japanese

lanuginosus, woolly
laevis, smooth
latifolius, broad-leaved
ligustrinus, privet-like
litoralis, of the sea-shore
lusitanicus, Portuguese
luteus, yellow
lycopodioides, like a club moss
lydius, of Lydia, Asia Minor

macrocarpus, with large fruits
major, greater
manipuliflorus, with flowers in little
    bundles
mediterraneus, Mediterranean, or
    from the middle of a land mass
minimus, smallest
minor, smaller
mollis, soft
mucronatus, sharp-pointed
multicolor, many coloured
multiflorus, many flowered
myrtillus, a small myrtle

nanus, dwarf
nidiformis, nest-shaped
niger, black
nitidus, shining
nudus, naked

obtusus, blunt
ochraceus, ochre-coloured
octopetalus, with eight petals
olympicus, from Mount Olympus

pallidus, pale
palmatus, with hand-like lobes
palustris, from the marsh
parviflorus, small-flowered
pendulus, pendulous, drooping
pilosus, very hairy
pinguifolius, with fat leaves
pisiferus, bearing pea-like cones
plenus, double-flowered
plumosus, feather-like
polifolius, with leaves like *Teucrium polium*
praecox, early flowering
procumbens, lying down
prostratus, prostrate, lying down
pubescens, soft-haired, downy
pulegioides, like *Mentha pulegium*
pulverulentus, powdered
purpureus, purple
pygmaeus, dwarf, very small
pyramidalis, pyramid-shaped

racemosus, arranged in a raceme
repandens, with wavy-edged leaves
repens, creeping
rigidus, stiff, inflexible
roseus, pinky red
rotundiflorus, with rounded flowers
ruber, red
rubrifolius, red-leaved
russatus, russet-coloured

sagittalis, with stems winged like the flights of an arrow
schizopetalus, with split corolla

scoparius, besom-like
scoticus, of Scotland
selaginoides, *Selaginella*-like
serpyllum, old name for thyme
speciosus, showy
spica, a spike
spiculifolius, with pointed leaves
splendens, shining, handsome
squamatus, scaly
strictus, rigid, stiff
suecicus, of Sweden
sylvestris, wild

taxifolius, with Yew-like leaves
tenuis, slender, delicate, thin
terminalis, with terminal flowers
tetragonus, quadrangular
tetralix, a classical twining plant
tinctorius, used by dyers
tomentosus, felted, woolly
tulipiferus, bearing tulip-shaped flowers

umbellatus, with flowers forming an umbel
uva-ursi, bear's grape

vagans, wandering
verrucosus, covered with warts
verticillatus, with leaves in whorls
villosus, shaggy
virens, *viridis*, green
viridiflorus, with green flowers
vitis-idaea, vine of Mount Ida – a Greek plant name
vulgaris, common

wisleyensis, of Wisley Garden

yakusimanus, of the island of Yakujima, Japan

Some Retail Nurseries for Hardy Heathers

British Isles

A. ANNABEL, Springwood, 22 Church Drive, Ravenshead, Nottingham.

MRS P. BENSON, Ridgeway Wood, Egton, Craven Arms, Shropshire.

ADRIAN BLOOM, Bressingham Gardens, Diss, Norfolk.

N. H. BRUMMAGE, Heathwood Nursery, Fakenham Road, Taverham, Norwich.

DAISY HILL NURSERIES, Newry, Co. Down, Northern Ireland.

P. DAVIS, Timber Tops, Marley Common, Haslemere, Surrey.

DELANEY & LYLE, Grange Nursery, Alloa, Clackmannan, Scotland.

DENBEIGH HEATHER NURSERIES, The Poplars, All Saints Road, Creeting St Mary, Ipswich, Suffolk.

JACK DRAKE, Inshriach Alpine Plant Nursery, Aviemore, Scotland.

EDROM NURSERIES, Coldingham, Berwickshire, Scotland.

D. & M. EVERETT, Mountpleasant Farm Nurseries, Elmley Lovett, Droitwich, Worcs.

G. M. HAMER, Sunnymount Nursery, Glossop Road, Chisworth, Hyde, Cheshire.

HARDWICKS NURSERIES, Newick, Lewes, Sussex.

HILLIER & SONS, Winchester, Hants.

G. G. HOLLETT, Greenbank Nursery, Sedbergh, Yorks.

HYDON NURSERIES, Clock Barn Lane, Hydon Heath, Godalming, Surrey.

W.E.TH. INGWERSEN, Birch Farm Nursery, Gravetye, E. Grinstead, Sussex.

KNAP HILL NURSERY, Barr's Lane, Knaphill, Woking, Surrey.

A. D. McFARLANE, Craigmarloch Nurseries, Barons Road, Rothesay, Bute, Scotland.

OLIVER & HUNTER, Moniaive, Thornhill, Dumfriesshire, Scotland.

G. OSMOND, Archfield Nursery, Wickwar, Wotton-under-Edge, Glos.

PENNYACRE NURSERIES, Crawley House, Springfield, Fife, Scotland.

L. R. RUSSELL, Richmond Nurseries, Windlesham, Surrey.

GERVASE SMITH, Hackney Road, Matlock, Derbys.

TABRAMHILL GARDENS, Ollerton Road, Arnold, Nottingham.

JOHN WATERER SONS & CRISP, Floral Mile, Twyford, Berks.

North America

AVALON MOUNTAIN GARDENS, Dana, N. Carolina 28724, USA.

JAMES CROSS, Box 824, Cutchoque, New York 11935, USA.

FLORA VISTA GARDENS, 4121 Rosedale Avenue, Vancouver, British Columbia, Canada.

MRS KNIGHT, Heather Acres, Rt 3, Box 231, Elma, Washington 98541, USA.

MANNING'S HEATHER FARM, 12450 Fiori Lane, Sebastopol, California 95472, USA.

W. M. STEWARD NURSERY, Rt 2, Box 225, Maple Valley, Washington 98038, USA.

SYLVAN NURSERY, 1028 Horseneck Road, S. Westport, Mass 02790, USA.

WESTON NURSERIES, Hopkinton, Mass 01748, USA.

Societies

THE HEATHER SOCIETY, c/o Harvest House, 62 London Road, Reading, Berks, England.

ERICULTURA, Heuvellaan 7, Hilversum, Holland.

GESELLSCHAFT DER HEIDEFREUNDE, Tangstedter Landstrasse 276, 2000 Hamburg 62, W. Germany.

Bibliography

Bean, W. J. (1970–3) – *Trees & Shrubs*, ed. 8, Vols 1 and 2. John Murray, London.

Beijerinck, W. (1940) – *Calluna, A Monograph on the Scotch Heather*. Verh. Kon. Ned. Akad. van Wetenschappen, 38(4).

Bloom, A. (1976) – *Guide to Garden Plants. 1. Heathers*. Jarrolds, Norwich.

Chapple, Fred. J. (1964) – *The Heather Garden*, 2nd revised edition.

Hansen, Irmgard (1950) – *Die europäischen Arten der Gattung Erica L.*; Bot. Jahrb. 75(1), 1–81.

Johnson, A. T. (1956) – *Hardy Heaths*.

Knight, F. P. (1972) Heaths & Heathers, Royal Horticultural Society, London

Laar, H. J. van de (1970) – *Calluna en Erica*; Dendroflora Nr. 7.

Letts, John F. (1966) – *Hardy Heaths and the Heather Garden*.

Maxwell, D. F. & Patrick, P. S. (1966) – *The English Heather Garden*.

McClintock, David (1969) – *A Guide to the Naming of Plants*, Heather Society.

McClintock, David (1971) – *Recent developments in the knowledge of European Ericas*; Bot. Jahrb. 90(4), 509–523.

Proudley, Brian & Valerie (1974) – *Heathers in Colour*, Blandford, London.

Underhill, Terry L. (1971) – *Heaths and Heathers*, David & Charles, Newton Abbott, Devon.

Webb, D. A. (1972) – *Ericaceae*, in Flora Europaea ed. T. G. Tutin, *et al.* Vol. 3, 5–13, Cambridge University Press.

Yates, G. (1978) *Pocket Guide to Heather Gardening*, 3rd Ed. Arnold, Nottingham.

Index of Cultivars

Where more than one page reference is given, the main entry is indicated in **bold** type.

General Index

MCCLINTOCK, DAVID
VAN DE LAAR, HARRY

MCCLINTOCK, DAVID
VAN DE LAAR, HARRY

DATE DUE	BORROWER'S NAME
7/7/87	Shirley Shinder
3/7/92	BRENDAN EARLS
12/22/03	Carl A. Neufour
5/29/05	